You Can Be FEARLESS

Live a Life Free From Fear

Fiona Inc.

www.fionainc.com

Published, April 2013
Fiona Inc.
www.fionainc.com
717-917-8101

Unless otherwise identified, Bible quotations in this book are from the Amplified and the King James versions of the Bible.

Special Thanks

I would like to thank my Lord and Savior Jesus, my Heavenly Father, and my greatest teacher, Holy Spirit.

My husband, Douglas, is an unending support to me. I am thankful that he leads me to do what God has called me to do. He spent many hours editing this book so that you could comprehend what I wanted to say. So thank you my love.

My wonderful sons Gabriel and Josiah, you are my cheerleaders and make life fun. I am thankful to be your mother.

Thanks to all of my wonderful family, friends and supporters. Without you my purpose would be obsolete.

Thank You!

Introduction

Fear is a tangible problem that faces many today. It is present in all walks of life and shows itself in the presence of the rich and poor. Fear likes to abide in the presence of people for it is there that it has its greatest expression.

But I have great news for you! You don't have to walk, live or think in fear anymore. You were created to dominate and eradicate fear. Fear must bow to you.

In this book we will examine the origin of fear, the environment that fear thrives in and the solutions that you can employ in your everyday life to give fear the boot once and for all.

You were created for greatness. In order to live a great life you should walk without weights that cause you to stumble, fall or get tired. Fear is a weight that brings with it friends of shame, condemnation, tiredness and a ton of other loads to cause you to become frustrated in life.

If you can be prevented from even trying, then you can be stopped from doing what you were created to do. But no more! You have the power and you will now have the plan you need to put fear in its place. Once and for all! Done, finished, the end!

You can be fearless every day, every hour, and every minute of your life. You were created for a greater purpose than to ward off fear, so let's get started.

Come and live again!

Fiona Pyszka

Contents

Foreword

I am very excited that God has called my wife to write this book. She is the epitome of a fearless person, a virtuous and anointed minister of the Lord. I am greatly inspired by her bold courage to overcome obstacles and limits. She is willing to take risks that many are not willing to take. Fiona is a woman who knows what she wants and goes after it with an unflinching, faith-filled belief that all things are possible to them that believe.

I have been married to her for almost sixteen years and have been an eye witness of her bold pursuit of excellence in all things. When she sets her mind to do something, it will be done well. She is a wonderful wife, a great mother, an anointed minister of the Lord, and a woman with impeccable integrity.

When she tells you that you can be fearless, you can listen to her because she lives a fearless life. We all need to be absolutely free from fear and this book will help you do just that.

After reading this book, you will not dream of being fearless anymore because you will become a fearless person who can do great exploits for the Lord. You can be fearless today.

Douglas Pyszka
Senior Pastor, Victory Christian Fellowship
Author – *"Depth"* – *Doing Excellent Principles of Truth with Honor*

Chapter One

The Fear Factor

You were created to be fearless, now walk confidently.

-Fiona Pyszka

That He would grant unto us, that we being delivered out of the hand of our enemies might serve Him without fear. - **Luke 1:74**

What is the real meaning of fear? Many people define fear based on their emotional feeling towards something. For example, someone might say, "I am so afraid of spiders," or "I hate snakes." These statements show feelings toward something, but do they capture the real definition of the word?

Fear is more than an impulse to run from a bug or reptile that looks deadly. It is more than the urge to hide when you see strangers. It is deeper than that. Its origin has more of a physical presence than we realize. It's not just an emotion; fear is a presence.

In fact, according to what we see in the book of Timothy, fear is a spirit and it did not come from our creator, God. Quite the opposite, instead of fear we were given three powerful gifts. Let's see what Timothy has to say:

1

2 Timothy 1:7 For God hath not given us the spirit of fear; but of power, and of love, and of a sound mind.

We can see from this passage that fear is a spirit. Even though a spirit cannot be seen, its presence can often times be felt. In order for fear to manifest itself publicly for all to see, it needs a body. It needs an expression vessel to show itself through. So when fearful emotions show up in people, they are being powered by a spirit called fear.

Do you get the picture? Can you see how people who live a lifestyle of fear become someone else when fear comes upon them? They get almost childlike in their behavior. Many phobias, disorders, and breakdowns are a result of the spirit of fear taking control of someone's life. This spirit leaves that person with a life of torture and uncertainty about the future.

There are popular reality shows now that display for all to see the devastating results of fear. For example, the show, "Hoarders," where a person is afraid to throw anything away, including trash. We see how fear has distorted their sense of reality. They cannot tell the difference between what is safe and unsafe, what is trash or what is treasure. They leave everything out to keep an eye on it, to help from losing anything.

What if the fear doesn't seem that bad for you? What if your fear is just about saying "hi" to a stranger? What if it's just about doing something new? You might say, "Those fears aren't a big deal. I can still live a very pleasant life without doing new things all the time or saying "hi" to everybody that passes by." Well of course you can, but the BIG question is, are you really doing what you're supposed to be doing? Is fear keeping you from doing what you were created to do?

Allowing little fears to thrive enables them to become greater vices for the future. Fear will not just come in and overpower you in a day; it stays around for a lifetime to have its way through you whenever it can.

But there is hope, as we see in the book of Timothy. God has given you another Spirit which promotes love, power and a sound mind. These are key ingredients to overcoming the power of the spirit of fear.

In later chapters, we will examine each of these characteristics of the Spirit God gave us. In the meantime, let's define fear and define what it means to be fearless.

According to the Merriam Webster's[1] dictionary, fear is defined as follows:

> *a : an unpleasant often strong emotion caused by anticipation or awareness of danger; b (1) : an instance of this emotion (2) : a state marked by this emotion; 2: anxious concern : solicitude; 3: profound reverence and awe especially toward God; 4: reason for alarm : danger*

We see in the middle of the definition the phrase, "profound reverence and awe ... toward God." However, for the purposes of this book we will define fear as a strong emotion towards danger with a reason for alarm, and anxious concern. Other words associated with fear that we will learn to overcome once and for all are "failure" and "rejection."

Fearlessness, on the other hand, is defined in the same dictionary as being "free from fear." That's a

---

[1] MERRIAM-WEBSTER ONLINE (www.Merriam-Webster.com) copyright © 2013 by Merriam-Webster, Incorporated.

powerful statement! You can live a life free from fear, or more accurately, free from the spirit of fear.

Before we move to the next chapter, take a moment to take inventory of things that hold you back. Leave the word "fear" out of the picture for a moment, and explore the following questions with me. Answer truthfully and thoroughly. Denial will only suppress the full freedom you can experience through this process.

Fearless Actions

1. What would I do, if I wasn't afraid of failing? ___

_____

_____

_____

_____

_____

_____

2. Who would I meet or talk to if I wasn't afraid of being rejected?_____

_____

_____

_____

_____

_____

3. What career decisions would I make if I wasn't afraid of being under qualified? _____

_____

Meditation[2]

It is very important after you have made your "fearless actions" list that you meditate on some words full of life. This will allow your mind to be renewed in areas that you have just exposed.

You have just done something that you might have never done before, exposing fears that have held you back. Now, don't leave without putting something fresh and alive in your mind. Here is a list of scriptures that I would encourage you to spend some time reviewing.

- **Joshua 1:8** This book of the law shall not depart out of thy mouth; but thou shalt meditate therein day and night, that thou mayest observe to do according to all that is written therein: for then thou shalt make thy

_____

[2] By meditation I mean to read out loud, then go over the words in your mind. Review each word individually. Give each word the opportunity to be "digested" for clarity and to be stored in your long term memory.

6

way prosperous, and then thou shalt have good success.

- **2 Timothy 1:7** For God hath not given us the spirit of fear; but of power, and of love, and of a sound mind.

- *Romans 8:15* For [the Spirit which] you have now received [is] not a spirit of slavery to put you once more in bondage to fear, but you have received the Spirit of adoption [the Spirit producing sonship] in [the bliss of] which we cry, Abba (Father)! Father!

.

Chapter Two
Mistaken Identity

Your identity was established before your birth. Don't let an enemy steal it from you now. - **Fiona Pyszka**
For the thing which I greatly fear comes upon me, and that of which I am afraid befalls me. - **Job 3:25**

Identity theft is a big deal these days. Entire companies have been established to combat the issue. It has now become part of the monthly overhead cost for businesses and homes to have security insurance to protect their identities. Our identity holds the power to give access to finances, determines our credit rating, and does a whole lot more. Because our identity is so valuable we take many steps to protect it. In the spiritual it is even more valuable, so we should protect it at all costs.

Spiritually, we have been given authority as believers in Jesus Christ. This authority was given to us to do great exploits and to accomplish much in the dimension of the kingdom of God. Jesus speaks of this in Luke:

9

Luke 10:19 I have given you authority to trample on snakes and scorpions and to overcome all the power of the enemy; nothing will harm you.

The thing about identity theft is that it doesn't always mean your entire identity is stolen. You still remain the same person you were, except your good name is now being used by someone else to destroy what you may have spent a lifetime building. In one day, your stolen identity could turn you from a successful person of integrity to a bankrupt pauper. This change is caused by decisions made by someone else using your identity. If a person knew about your good success yesterday, then saw your bankruptcy today without knowing what had happened, they might be wondering what you could have done that was so wrong.

The story of Job in the Bible is a good example of this. The Bible describes Job as a righteous and blameless man. Then it lists his portfolio as owning much and having many children. He was a wealthy, healthy, God-fearing man. His identity was one to be envied by many (Job 1:1). Then, in one day, everything changed.

10

By chapter two, Job has turned into someone who dreads the day he was born. He loses his health, his wealth, and his family. Now he is having conversations with his friends to defend why he lost everything. They each have several reasons to share with him as to why this entire calamity has occurred. They each have their own view of who God is and how God is punishing Job for something. However, we see that God Himself identifies Job as a righteous man: "There is no one on earth like him; he is blameless and upright, a man who fears God and shuns evil" (Job 1:8). How could such a stellar report from God result in such a devastating life in a matter of days? In less than a week, Job goes from being God's poster child of blessing to the laughing stock of the city. His wife even urges him to "curse God and die" (Job 2:9).

Job's identity was changed. Anyone who heard of this new Job would certainly think that there must have been some mistaken identity. This could not be the same man who was well-revered and highly esteemed, the richest man in the east, the one who helped others. This could not be the same man, but he was!

So what happened? Let's take a closer look. We discover a clue to how Job lost his identity,

> *Job 3:25 For the thing which I greatly feared is come upon me, and that which I was afraid of is come unto me.*

We see in this verse that Job had a part to play in what came upon him. He gave fear power to pull towards him the wrath of Satan. Satan was trying to dare God to take negative action and show God that the loyalty of this great man would be changed when he no longer had God's blessings to rely on.

We see here that Job was blessed by God and Satan was asking God to take His blessings from Job, thinking that this would Job's righteousness.

> *Job 1:7 – 12 And the LORD said unto Satan, Whence comest thou? Then Satan answered the LORD, and said, From going to and fro in the earth, and from walking up and down in it.*
>
> *[8] And the LORD said unto Satan, Hast thou considered my servant Job, that there is none like him in the earth, a perfect and an upright man, one that feareth God, and escheweth evil?*
>
> *[9] Then Satan answered the LORD, and said, Doth Job fear God for nought?*

¹⁰ Hast not thou made an hedge about him, and about his house, and about all that he hath on every side? thou hast blessed the work of his hands, and his substance is increased in the land.

¹¹ But put forth thine hand now, and touch all that he hath, and he will curse thee to thy face.

¹² And the LORD said unto Satan, Behold, all that he hath is in thy power; only upon himself put not forth thine hand. So Satan went forth from the presence of the LORD.

Wow, what an intense discussion between God and Satan. This could be viewed as an epic showdown between God and Satan. God presents Job as His most honorable servant on earth, perfect and upright and one who has fear and respect for God. The fear that God talks about here is the reverential awe of who God is and how great Job thought God was.

But there was another fear brewing. Job admits that the things that came upon him are the things he was afraid of. The New Living Bible version puts it this way,

Job 3:25 What I always feared has happened to me. What I dreaded has come true.

Because Job yielded to the spirit of fear, Satan had an opening and a right to mess with Job's affairs. The only stipulation was that Satan could not kill Job. Do you see how devastating a little fear can be? Here was a man that was an example of God's blessings, yet because of his fear issue he gave Satan an opportunity to devour him. We see in this story that all Satan wants to do is to cause destruction. Satan thinks that everyone has his nature, a nature of only having relationships for what you can get out of them. What he encountered though is a relationship with a God-fearing man and his God. What I find interesting in this story is that Job really was the most God-fearing man of his time. Others around him suggested that he curse God, even his wife urged him to curse God and die, and his friends sure didn't know the truth about God's mercy and how He operated.

We see that Job's language then became very stout against God. Then God came on the scene and asked Job to answer His questions (Job 38). He had very sobering questions for Job, asking him where he was when God stretched out the sky in its creation, or if Job was there when God created His biggest animals. You get the idea. Job was God's most honoring and awestruck servant, yet his yielding to the spirit of fear caused him to be sidetracked, sick, broke, and disgusted with life. Giving into a small fear opened the door for big destruction.

It's not enough to honor God. If you entertain the spirit of fear in your life, as Job did, you leave yourself vulnerable even while you're worshiping and respecting God. The spirit of fear has no respect for the presence of God when a person has given it access. This spirit does not mind hanging out with you while you worship God, because it knows that it can have access again when you're all finished.

Once you give access to the spirit of fear, its goal and plans are to take control of you. It doesn't matter how long it takes for the agenda of this spirit to be fulfilled, it will plug away, wear you down and plan how it will take over your life and infiltrate your family line for generations to come.

But God's help is always at hand. When we recognize it and ask for it, He steps in. Job finally came to this realization. Let's take a look.

> *Job 42:8-10 Now therefore take seven bullocks and seven rams and go to My servant Job and offer up for yourselves a burnt offering; and My*

servant Job shall pray for you, for I will accept [his prayer] that I deal not with you after your folly, in that you have not spoken of Me the thing that is right, as My servant Job has.

⁹ So Eliphaz the Temanite and Bildad the Shuhite and Zophar the Naamathite went and did as the Lord commanded them; and the Lord accepted [Job's prayer].

¹⁰ And the Lord turned the captivity of Job and restored his fortunes, when he prayed for his friends; also the Lord gave Job twice as much as he had before.

Job was right to fight through and defend what God had given him. The fear that Job walked in did not have the final say. Even if you've made a mistake and allowed fear to enter your life and have a voice, even if it has made you take actions that has caused a breach in your life, this does not have to be the end of the story. Fear can be told to go bye-bye. It can be given the boot. How do we do that? We do it by listening to God's instructions and moving on from there.

Job had fear of his children sinning when they partied, so, in order to not have them be defiled or live against God, he was always making sacrifices on their behalf to God.

> *Job 1:4-5 His sons used to go and feast in the house of each on his day (birthday) in turn, and they invited their three sisters to eat and drink with them.*
>
> *5 And when the days of their feasting were over, Job sent for them to purify and hallow them, and rose up early in the morning and offered burnt offerings according to the number of them all. For Job said, It may be that my sons have sinned and cursed or disowned God in their hearts. Thus did Job at all [such] times.*

This is a fear move. It's a move that says "just in case something happens, I am going to do this." It puts contingency plans in place to protect against things that are perceived may happen.

Don't get me wrong, strategic planning for your future is great and necessary in everyone's life. However, confessing sins or asking forgiveness for sins that are perceived to have happened or will happen is a whole different story. Job ended up losing the very children he was sacrificing to protect. Job himself acknowledged that what he feared had come upon him (Job 3:25).

The spirit of fear manifested to steal, kill and destroy what Job had. When you realize, as Job did, that it could be your own fear that has caused some things to happen in your life, you are in place for a turnaround. It means that God can give you an instruction to move on. As long as you keep mulling over why God has done this to you, you will be stuck in a zone of defeat and hopelessness. Job was honored for not agreeing with his three friends who had all the wrong reasons why Job was experiencing this harm.

> *Job 42:7-8 After the Lord had spoken the previous words to Job, the Lord said to Eliphaz the Temanite, My wrath is kindled against you and against your two friends, for you have not spoken of Me the thing that is right, as My servant Job has.*
>
> *⁸ Now therefore take seven bullocks and seven rams and go to My servant Job and offer up for yourselves a burnt offering; and My servant Job shall pray for you, for I will accept [his prayer] that I deal not with you after your folly, in that you have not spoken of Me the thing that is right, as My servant Job has.*

As you can see, God instructed Job to pray for his friends because God said He would accept his prayer. Why didn't God accept Job's prayer for his children?

Job's sacrifices for his children were done in the spirit of fear. He was anticipating things that they might have done. He was fearful that they might have sinned against God, so he was taking their place to cover up what they might have done. Job seemed to have missed the point that we are each responsible for our own behaviors before God. Job's children were the ones who should have been sacrificing. Be careful how you might be trying to cover up for someone in your life who should be taking responsibility for their own actions. Your cover up could be an instruction from the spirit of fear and not from the Spirit of God. Big difference!

We see that the end of Job's story was greater than the beginning of his sorrows. God restored double what was taken from him because of the spirit of fear. God knows how to answer the spirit of fear and turn its destruction into blessing. God knows how to come in and answer with multiplication if we will let Him. Job did what God asked him to do: he prayed for his friends, and then restoration occurred.

Job 42:15-17 And in all the land there were no women so fair as the daughters of Job, and their father gave them inheritance among their brothers.

[16] After this, Job lived 140 years, and saw his sons and his sons' sons, even to four generations.

[17] So Job died, an old man and full of days.

At the end of his life, Job died a man full of days and lived to see his grandchildren to the fourth generation. How awesome! Only Satan will come in and attack you and then condemn you for it. God doesn't want to condemn when fear is let in, He wants to restore. It doesn't matter what fear factor you have let in your life today, you can ask God to rescue you and the things that were lost through fear can now be restored double.

Enjoy your double now!

Fearless Actions

1. Is there any area of your life you feel has been opened to fear? If so, pray now to ask God for an instruction to get you back on track. Write His instructions down and don't neglect to follow them_____

_____

_____

_____

_____

_____

_____

_____

_____

_____

_____

_____

Meditation

Here are some scriptures for you to meditate on regarding not fearing for your family or children.

- Hebrews 2:13 And again He says, My trust and assured reliance and confident hope shall be fixed in Him. And yet again, Here I am, I and the children whom God has given Me.

- Hebrews 2:14 Since, therefore, [these His] children share in flesh and blood [in the physical nature of human beings], He [Himself] in a similar manner partook of the same [nature], that by [going through] death He

21

might bring to nought and make of no effect him who had the power of death—that is, the devil.

- Hebrews 2:15 And also that He might deliver and completely set free all those who through the [haunting] fear of death were held in bondage throughout the whole course of their lives.

- Hebrews 2:16 For, as we all know, He [Christ] did not take hold of angels [the fallen angels, to give them a helping and delivering hand], but He did take hold of [the fallen] descendants of Abraham [to reach out to them a helping and delivering hand].

Chapter Three
The Fearless Among Us

Neither age nor circumstances can stop the fearless.

*- **Fiona Pyszka***

But the people who know their God shall prove themselves strong and shall stand firm and do exploits [for God]. - **Daniel 11:32**

The story of David and Goliath is my son Gabriel's favorite Bible story. When he was a little boy he would act out his favorite scene with his dad. He would always be David and his dad got the privilege of being Goliath. Gabriel's favorite part was saying, "You come at me with a sword, but I come at you in the name of the Lord."

> *1 Samuel 17:45 David said to the Philistine, "You come against me with sword and spear and javelin, but I come against you in the name of the Lord Almighty, the God of the armies of Israel, whom you have defied.*

Here, David passionately expresses how Goliath is defying God by his very words against God's people. Isn't that what's really happening today? When fear comes in, it is in direct opposition to God's people, what God can do for them, and, even worse, what God's power in them can accomplish. We see in this heroic story of David and Goliath how Goliath opposed God, and God won. .

Let's take a closer look at the story of David and Goliath. We see an entire army, trained for battle and led by a great king, stand fearfully watching as one giant mouths off about what his plan was for them. He hadn't yet done a thing. All he was doing was talking.

> *1 Samuel 17:8 -11 Goliath stood and shouted to the ranks of Israel, Why have you come out to draw up for battle? Am I not a Philistine, and are you not servants of Saul? Choose a man for yourselves and let him come down to me.*

> *9 If he is able to fight with me and kill me, then we will be your servants; but if I prevail against him and kill him, then you shall be our servants and serve us.*

> *10 And the Philistine said, I defy the ranks of Israel this day; give me a man, that we may fight together.*

> *11 When Saul and all Israel heard those words of the Philistine, they were dismayed and greatly afraid.*

As part of his fear strategy, Goliath stood out, came forward and changed the terms of the war. He decided that instead of an army-to-army battle it would be a one-on-one fight. He stood there with all of his armor and weapons, and decided that if any one person in the Israelite army could overcome his strength and his power, then they would win.

The truth is there was an entire army available to fight the Philistine army. No matter how the Philistines decided to present their army to fight, the military strategy of Israel did not need to change. I believe if Israel's entire army had stopped wondering which one of them could fight this Goliath, and instead thought of how all of them could fight him, they would have won without fear. Instead, they were trapped by the spirit of fear and they thought on the enemy's terms.

You don't have to play by fear's rules. You don't have to fight fear alone. You can rise up and fight with the army that is at your disposal. You have an army at your disposal. When you become part of the body of Christ you have family that will fight with you. Sometimes, people forget this because they are kept isolated by their fear. It's one of the tactics of the spirit of fear. Fear's aim is to get you isolated and have you fight one-on-one while he taunts you with words, only words. The things that you are taunted with have not yet happened, they are just "what-ifs." The goal, when you fight fear, is to win. You don't have to win fear by fighting one-on-one, you just have to win. So bring in all the resources, weapons, and words that are available to you. Always remember fear is always trying to prevent you from having something greater in your life. If you spend your whole life fighting one fear, then you miss the entire purpose of what you should be doing to begin with.

No matter what the threat is, be familiar with your weapons and know how to use them. We see in the story of David and Goliath that an army was fearful, but a young man knew who his God was.

Here is a fearless principle for you: you MUST know who your God is and what He is capable of doing for you. David was appalled at this uncircumcised Philistine who defied the armies of the Living God. It was the defilement of God's army that caused David to ask questions of why an army was standing there while a non-covenant man stood taunting them.

1 Samuel 17:26 And David said to the men standing by him, What shall be done for the man who kills this Philistine and takes away the reproach from Israel? For who is this uncircumcised Philistine that he should defy the armies of the living God?

David was coming in to do something that grown men, trained for battle were not able to do. This win carried with it a reward. David wanted to make sure that he knew what the reward was. Note here, whenever you defeat a Goliath of fear in your life, always expect to receive the benefits of the victory. There should always be a reward and many times more than one. When fear decides to show up in your life, don't just let it leave without paying. It has to leave something behind that is valuable to you.

David caused an entire army to run away from the Israelites after he defeated their champion.

1 Samuel 17:51-53 . . .When the Philistines saw that their mighty champion was dead, they fled.

52 And the men of Israel and Judah rose with a shout and pursued the Philistines as far as Gath and the gates of Ekron. So the wounded Philistines fell along the way from Shaaraim as far as Gath and Ekron.

27

53 The Israelites returned from their pursuit of the Philistines and plundered their tents.

This little teenage boy caused a breakthrough for the elite soldiers of Israel. He caused them to step out and finish the war, securing the spoil. As a result, he became a member of the royal family by marrying the king's daughter, he became rich, and his family was exempt from paying taxes. David is a great example of someone fearless.

> *1 Samuel 17:25 And the Israelites said, Have you seen this man who has come out? Surely he has come out to defy Israel; and the man who kills him the king will enrich with great riches, and will give him his daughter and make his father's house free [from taxes and service] in Israel.*

Another good example of a fearless person in the Bible is Esther. She became queen of a kingdom in which she was a foreigner. However she was there at the right time for the right reason. Her resistance to fear didn't protect only her; it protected God's chosen people.

Esther's uncle, Mordecai, asked her to present to the king a case to save God's people. We see in the passage below her explanation to her uncle that it had been more than thirty days since the king had asked to see her. She had to rise above the fear that the king would put to death anyone who entered his presence uninvited.

> *Esther 4:11 All the king's servants and the people of the king's provinces know that any person, be it man or woman, who shall go into the inner court to the king without being called shall be put to death; there is but one law for him, except [him] to whom the king shall hold out the golden scepter, that he may live. But I have not been called to come to the king for these thirty days.*

These were all facts that would cause people to be afraid and not take action. Fear was saying to Esther, "Who do you think you are? If you enter the king's inner court uninvited the law dictates that you die, instantly." Fear was trying to stop Esther from taking actions to save her people. She was one person; what could she do? Was she willing to take the risk of being politically incorrect, and would she overcome the boundaries that fear was trying to keep her in? In order to defy fear and be fearless, you need to step over boundaries, defy man-made laws of bondage, and initiate change that may have never been seen before. That's exactly what Esther did in her reply to her uncle Mordecai. Here we see the conversation between them.

> *Esther 4:13-17 Then Mordecai told them to return this answer to Esther, Do not flatter yourself that you shall escape in the king's palace any more than all the other Jews.*
>
> *[14] For if you keep silent at this time, relief and deliverance shall arise for the Jews from elsewhere, but you and your father's house will perish. And who knows but that you have come to the kingdom for such a time as this and for this very occasion?*
>
> *[15] Then Esther told them to give this answer to Mordecai,*
>
> *[16] Go, gather together all the Jews that are present in Shushan, and fast for me; and neither eat nor drink for three days, night or day. I also and my maids will fast as you do. Then I will go to the king, though it is against the law; and if I perish, I perish.*
>
> *[17] So Mordecai went away and did all that Esther had commanded him.*

Possibly, the most famous phrase from this discourse would be in verse 16 where Esther states, "If I perish, I perish." She was determined to appear before the king. She knew that the only way to stop the demise of her people and to capture the man, Haman, who had perpetrated this evil plot against the Jews, was to speak to the king. She would have to resist fear and approach the king. This was her husband, the man she was married to. Yet, she was so afraid of the law of the land that she was afraid to approach him to ask him to do something in his power to help her and her people.

What has the spirit of fear prevented you from accomplishing in your own life? Who has the spirit of fear made you afraid of? Are you afraid to have conversations with family members? Are you afraid of arresting family fears that could cause the demise of future generations?

Because Esther overcame the plans of the spirit of fear, she made a big difference in the country. Not only did she not die, but neither did any of her people. As a matter of fact, Haman was hanged on the same gallows he had made to kill the Jews. The people of the land all wanted to be Jews when they saw the great victory the Jews secured for themselves. All because the queen, a young lady, was not afraid to speak to her husband, the king of a nation, to spare the lives of her native people.

> Esther 7:10 So they hanged Haman on the gallows that he had prepared for Mordecai. Then the king's wrath was pacified.
>
> Esther 8:16-17 The Jews had light [a dawn of new hope] and gladness and joy and honor.
>
> ¹⁷ And in every province and in every city, wherever the king's command and his decree came, the Jews had gladness and joy, a feast and a holiday. And many from among the peoples of the land [submitted themselves to Jewish rite and] became Jews, for the fear of the Jews had fallen upon them.

One act of bravery, an act of defiance against the spirit of fear, and God's chosen people were saved. They received their dignity back and people wanted to be like them. One orphan girl became queen and changed the fate of a nation.

All of this could not have happened had she given into the spirit of fear, wrapped around the traditions and laws of men. Man-made lows that defy God's truth are brought about by the spirit of fear. These laws are fear-based, otherwise no one would follow them. If you find yourself doing something because you're afraid of what might happen to you or your family if you don't comply, then get out from that situation. Defy it. You heard me right: defy manmade laws or bondages that cause you to hurt your future, what God has asked you to do.

There are many more instances in the Bible of people who defied the law of the land to serve and defend the truth of God. We will explore these a little more in the chapters ahead.

Fearless Actions

1. Are there any traditions of men from your community, culture, or background that have made you afraid of doing what you know you should be doing for God? Write them down. _

_____

_____

_____

_____

2. Ask God for a plan to get out from under the pressure and bondage of those fears. Write down His answers to you._____

_____

_____

3. Make your statement of not turning back here, Esther's was, "If I perish, I perish." _____

_____

_____

_____

4. Write the picture of freedom you see from defying the fear that has held you back. How will things be different from now on? Write it down, paint a picture with words. _____

_____

_____

_____

_____

_____

Meditation

Mediate on these scriptures as you spend time evaluating your current situation. Fasting during this time would be a good addition as well. If you read the story of Esther further, you'll find that she called a three-day fast before she went to see the king.

- Joshua 1:9 Have I not commanded you? Be strong and courageous. Do not be afraid; do not be discouraged, for the Lord your God will be with you wherever you go."

- Joshua 14:11 I am still as strong today as the day Moses sent me out; I'm just as vigorous to go out to battle now as I was then.
- Luke 11:21 When a strong man, fully armed, guards his own house, his possessions are safe.

Chapter Four

The Strongest Weapon of the Fearless

"When you speak, you should expect what you say to happen"- **Fiona Pyszka**

"Out of the mouths of babes and unweaned infants You have established strength because of Your foes, that You might silence the enemy and the avenger."

– Psalm 8:2

"Sticks and stones may break my bones but names will never hurt me." Remember hearing that rhyme growing up? This popular children's rhyme was meant to help people not be affected by being bullied with words. Yet, it seems this very popular rhyme has missed its intention. Today, as I help many people discover and walk towards fulfilling their purpose, I have noticed the number one obstacle that has blocked people has been words or name calling they have experienced in their life.

Words are containers and their value is based on who speaks them. In the New Testament, we read these words spoken to a young lady named Mary:

> *Luke 1: 30 And the angel said unto her, Fear not, Mary: for thou hast found favour with God.*

37

³¹ And, behold, thou shalt conceive in thy womb, and bring forth a son, and shalt call his name JESUS.

³⁴ Then said Mary unto the angel, How shall this be, seeing I know not a man?

³⁵ And the angel answered and said unto her, The Holy Ghost shall come upon thee, and the power of the Highest shall overshadow thee: therefore also that holy thing which shall be born of thee shall be called the Son of God.

Mary was impregnated with the seed of the Holy Spirit simply because she received the words spoken to her by the angel Gabriel. Imagine this: the Savior of the world was brought into being through words spoken to the womb of a young virgin. She received God's Word fearlessly and brought forth a child named Jesus.

Before Jesus' ministry years, the people were used to hearing only from the high priests. These priests would perform the traditions of serving God by speaking phrases that were learned, passed down through traditions of men. But all of these words were spoken as mere traditions. There was no power in their words because they were doing a ceremonial action. But then one day another priest came on the scene and started speaking. Here is what happened when Jesus entered the synagogue.

> *Luke 4:14-22 Then Jesus went back full of and under the power of the [Holy] Spirit into Galilee, and the fame of Him spread through the whole region round about.*
>
> *15 And He Himself conducted [a course of] teaching in their synagogues, being recognized and honored and praised by all.*
>
> *16 So He came to Nazareth, [that Nazareth] where He had been brought up, and He entered the synagogue, as was His custom on the Sabbath day. And He stood up to read.*
>
> *17 And there was handed to Him [the roll of] the book of the prophet Isaiah. He opened (unrolled) the book and found the place where it was written,*
>
> *18 The Spirit of the Lord [is] upon Me, because He has anointed Me [the Anointed One, the Messiah] to preach the good news (the Gospel) to the poor; He has sent Me to announce release to the captives and recovery of sight to the blind, to send forth as delivered those who*

are oppressed [who are downtrodden, bruised, crushed, and broken down by calamity],

19 To proclaim the accepted and acceptable year of the Lord [the day when salvation and the free favors of God profusely abound].

20 Then He rolled up the book and gave it back to the attendant and sat down; and the eyes of all in the synagogue were gazing [attentively] at Him.

21 And He began to speak to them: Today this Scripture has been fulfilled while you are present and hearing.

22 And all spoke well of Him and marveled at the words of grace that came forth from His mouth; and they said, Is not this Joseph's Son?

When Jesus stood up to read, His words were powerful! It was different than any other reading they had heard in the synagogue. We see in verse 22 that "all spoke well of Him and marveled at the words of grace that came forth from His mouth." His mouth power had them marveling. They were even asking if this was the son of Joseph.

The people did not marvel that the book of Isaiah was being read, and they weren't marveling that there was a scripture reading in synagogue that day. They marveled at the authority with which it was read. Later in that verse, with another group, we see the same response to Jesus' spoken word to demons.

> *Luke 4:36 All the people were amazed and said to each other, "What words these are! With authority and power he gives orders to impure spirits and they come out!"*

What makes Jesus' words so powerful? There is one ingredient that causes a person's words to be powerful instead of mere wishful thinking. A fearless person's words carry a heavy weight of authority. They expect that when they say something it happens. They don't consider their words imposing on someone or on traditions. They believe that what they say will happen. Jesus had this authority when He spoke because of how He treated His heavenly Father.

So what is this one ingredient mixed with our words that gives it a high value? It is the one thing that pleases God. What pleases God? Hebrews tells us:

> *Hebrews 11:6 And without faith it is impossible to please God, because anyone who comes to*

him must believe that he exists and that he rewards those who earnestly seek him.

From this passage we see that faith is necessary for our ways to please God. Without faith, thinking of pleasing God is a vain thought.

Jesus pleased His Father, and God spoke publicly about how pleased He was with Jesus.

> *Matthew 3:17 And lo a voice from heaven, saying, This is my beloved Son, in whom I am well pleased.*

We know that faith pleases God, so another important thing to know is how we can get or build faith. The Bible reveals how we get and build faith. We see it here in Romans:

> *Romans 10:17 So then faith cometh by hearing, and hearing by the word of God.*

Faith is attracted by hearing God's words. This means that we should not be listening to the words of fear. We should not hear the whispers of evil, the sounds that tell you what you are unable to do or say and what is impossible.

Faith is attracted to words that breathe life, and faith grows with life-filled words. The only words that can multiply more life is the word of Almighty God. He has given us so many fruitful words that we could spend our entire lifetime chewing on these words that build our faith to major strength. The great thing about faith is that you just need a little bit to move big things.

> *Matthew 17:20 He said to them, Because of the littleness of your faith [that is, your lack of firmly relying trust]. For truly I say to you, if you have faith [that is living] like a grain of mustard seed, you can say to this mountain, Move from here to yonder place, and it will move; and nothing will be impossible to you.*

> *Luke 17:6 And the Lord answered, If you had faith (trust and confidence in God) even [so small] like a grain of mustard seed, you could say to this mulberry tree, Be pulled up by the roots, and be planted in the sea, and it would obey you.*

It wasn't the size of the faith that mattered, it was the potency of the faith, based on the Person of Christ who authored it. Living words will produce a vibrant life. The creation of a human starts with cells multiplying. A mustard seed doesn't stay a seed after it is planted in the right soil; it grows as it receives light, water and proper care.

43

You must see your words as something to protect and care for. You must see your words as faith vessels, full of life, and seeds capable of producing fruit. How do you do this? You must speak truthful words. Wishful thinking is not truthful words; it is the speech of a gambler. It's like throwing a dice, hoping for the best.

When you speak words of life and stand by them, you are not afraid when the answer comes. Faith arises when you hear words of life. You must know when words come from your Father in heaven and when they come from your enemy. If you are not able to understand the difference between your enemy and God you could end up living a frustrating life of fear. A life where you are never sure if God is leading you or if the devil is trying to trick you. Here is what Jesus had to say to those who did not operate in faith.

> Matthew 8:26 And he saith unto them, Why are ye fearful, O ye of little faith? Then he arose, and rebuked the winds and the sea; and there was a great calm.

Jesus considered fearfulness as having little faith, which is faith that has such a low frequency of power that it could not stop the biggest storm they were facing at the moment. In the passage we see the disciples were traveling in a boat while Jesus slept, and they encountered a storm. He was awakened to take care of a problem that the disciples' mouths were not capable of handling because their faith was weakened by fear.

In another story, we see a priest in the New Testament who couldn't believe how God answered him and his wife's prayer. His answer came to him in God's house while he was performing his priestly duty. He was in the synagogue burning incense to God, and his wife was at home. She was not in the presence of her husband when an angel gave him the answer to their prayer. Let's take a look at the conversation between the angel and Zachariah.

> Luke 1:13 But the angel said to him, Do not be afraid, Zachariah, because your petition was heard, and your wife Elizabeth will bear you a son, and you must call his name John [God is favorable].

Reading on, we see that Zachariah's answer was full of fear, doubt and unbelief – even though he had prayed for this very thing with his wife. We see his answer to the angel here,

Luke 1:18 And Zachariah said to the angel, By what shall I know and be sure of this? For I am an old man, and my wife is well advanced in years.

His answer proved that he was just playing along with a request from his wife. It didn't seem that he believed his own prayer request. He was asking the angel how he was to be sure of this. Imagine praying for something with confidence, but when the answer comes you say, "I don't believe that this is possible." Here's the big question, if you didn't believe it in the first place, then why did you say it? Many people throw out fearful words in prayer all the time. We know it's in fear because when the answer comes, they don't recognize it. If you speak something into existence, then you should know what it looks like when it shows up. You should at least recognize the product. What you might not know is how or when it will come, but when it comes you should definitely know that it was your words that manifested it before you. It is similar to when someone plants an apple tree. They would never deny the apples on a tree when the harvest shows up. If you know you planted apples then you are excited when apples show up.

46

So what happened to this priest in the house of God who questioned the answer to his own request? Here is the response to his unbelief:

> *Luke 1:18-20 And the angel replied to him, I am Gabriel. I stand in the [very] presence of God, and I have been sent to talk to you and to bring you this good news.*
>
> *20 Now behold, you will be and will continue to be silent and not able to speak till the day when these things take place, because you have not believed what I told you; but my words are of a kind which will be fulfilled in the appointed and proper time.*

The angel Gabriel believed his own words, as we see in verse 20, "My words are of a kind which will be fulfilled." Are you so confident in your words that you have consequences for people who dare to question or think of them lightly? The angel Gabriel spoke God's words and placed high value in them. He fearlessly defended the message he was sent to deliver. If you are fearful you will allow people to glaze over your words and make light and fun of what you're saying. But if you are fearless you will correct with consequences those who dare to question the word of God that you speak. When your words originate from the source of truth, God, you will believe strongly what you say because you know the source from where it comes.

The source of your words is important because what backs your words authorizes your words. It has to be more than self-will and positive speaking. It has to be faith speaking. Faith is a word that should be an absolute staple in your vocabulary.

Zachariah's story ended well. His wife, Elizabeth, received what she believed for, a son. He was named John, just like the angel said, and he became everything the angel Gabriel said he would be.

The value you place on your words will determine the level of fearlessness you enjoy in life. Fearlessness is more than an occasional experience; it must become part of who you are at all times in every situation.

Fearless Actions

1. Rate your word value from 1-10 with 10 being the highest. Do you place a high value on what you say now? _____

_____

_____

_____

2. List some areas where you might have devalued your words and reaped negative results from the experience. _____

_____

_____

_____

3. List areas where you have valued your words and they have come to pass and yielded positive results in your life. _____

_____

_____

_____

4. Now analyze the difference in your results between questions 2 and 3. List what you need to change to have your words become more valuable. _____

_____

_____

Meditation

scriptures to help build your faith are listed below. Meditate on them with the expectation that the value of what you say will increase as you learn how to study the word of God and apply it in your everyday speaking.

- Matthew 9:29 . . .saying, According to your faith be it unto you.
- Mark 11:22 And Jesus answering saith unto them, Have faith in God.
- Romans 4:20 He staggered not at the promise of God through unbelief; but was strong in faith, giving glory to God.
- Romans 10:8 But what saith it? The word is nigh thee, even in thy mouth, and in thy heart: that is, the word of faith, which we preach.
- Romans 10:17 So then faith cometh by hearing, and hearing by the word of God.
- 1 Corinthians 2:5 That your faith should not stand in the wisdom of men, but in the power of God.
- Hebrews 10:38 Now the just shall live by faith: but if any man draw back, my soul shall have no pleasure in him.

Chapter Five
Fearlessly Bold

"To be bold is to stand firm knowing who is backing you up" – **Fiona Pyszka**
"The wicked flee though no one pursues, but the righteous are as bold as a lion." – **Proverbs 28:1**

I live in a home with three handsome men. I call my two young sons "men" because I speak to their future. They are very much into the boy stuff, but respect and love mommy enough to indulge my many female needs for a good "girly" movie or TV show. However, there have been several occasions when we've watched shows about predators and prey.

I must admit, it is quite eye opening and educational to see the many facets of the animal kingdom. An animal that we like to learn about is the lion. It is a predator that will not let anything get in its way of food, shelter, or rest. Lions know how to protect their young and are always on guard for attacks from other predators.

We see the lion highly feared in the animal kingdom. The lion is often called the king of the jungle. You never see a lion having to muster up the nerve to go to a fight, because lions were created for the fight. They never back down and they always fight with the intention of bringing back spoil. The lion always intends to win, and when they show up to a fight they are ready to conquer.

There is a certain fierceness that is seen in the eyes and stance of a lion. Lions have created a reputation for themselves. They are known around the world for their power and authority in the jungle and their boldness when facing opponents.

The Bible tells us to be as bold as a lion.

> *Proverbs 28:1 The wicked flee when no man pursueth: but the righteous are bold as a lion.*

When we read this scripture, we need to create an image of someone standing bold as a lion not fleeing like the wicked. We must be known for having a reputation of boldness anywhere we go. It must become your natural instinct. To develop that kind of reputation, we must begin to act boldly and fearlessly. This verse in Proverbs shows us that wicked people flee, but the righteous are as bold as a lion. They stand, defend, and speak to situations until they have won. Here is another verse that talks about standing:

Ephesians 6:13 Wherefore take unto you the whole armour of God, that ye may be able to withstand in the evil day, and having done all, to stand.

Standing requires sure-footedness and sober-mindedness. It is difficult for someone who is drunk to stand straight or upright for a long period of time. The Bible tells us to be sober-minded. Being bold as a lion, standing strong, and being sober-minded are three nuggets of truth that, when combined, help you live a fearless life.

1 Peter 5:8 Be alert and of sober mind. Your enemy the devil prowls around like a roaring lion looking for someone to devour.

The lion in this verse is not a real lion, but Satan trying to be a lion, mimicking the characteristics of Jesus, the Lion of the Tribe of Judah. When you are aware of the devil's devices, then you know to ignore his roaring and be sober-minded to stand in your boldness. Never back down when fear shows up roaring. Face it boldly and you will win. You must stay focused and stand. Set your face as flint, not moving nor shaking, and speak consistently powerful words of life.

Isaiah 50:7 For the Lord God helps me;
therefore have I not been ashamed or
confounded. Therefore have I set my face like a
flint, and I know that I shall not be put to shame.

You must move forward in what you say and the decisions you make without shame or confusion. You must have your face set like flint. If you give in to the enemy's tactics and his fearful words, then you are giving in to a fake lion that has learned how to sound like the real thing. You must remember that you are supposed to be as bold as a lion, the real thing. Besides you are part of the tribe of the Lion of Judah, and being part of a tribe has its benefits.

Revelation 5:5 And one of the elders saith unto
me, Weep not: behold, the Lion of the tribe of
Judah, the Root of David, hath prevailed to open
the book, and to loose the seven seals thereof.

Having like-minded people surrounding you gives you security. Jesus is the Lion of the tribe of Judah, which means that we are also lions with Him. Since we are part of the tribe that He is a part of, we are entitled to what He is entitled to, and we get to benefit from the word that He has fulfilled. All of this is summed up in this verse:

Romans 8:17 And if children, then heirs; heirs of God, and joint-heirs with Christ; if so be that we suffer with him, that we may be also glorified together.

We are joint heirs with Jesus and that means that we get to participate in His family. See yourself as a lion or lioness in the Kingdom of God. You might be considering this as somewhat of a weird scenario. You may be thinking, "What difference does it make it I see myself as a lion or not?" I'm glad you asked. Let's look at a group of people who saw themselves as less than their opponent.

Numbers 13:33 And there we saw the giants, the sons of Anak, which come of the giants: and we were in our own sight as grasshoppers, and so we were in their sight.

You must see yourself as a lion not as a grasshopper. The children of Israel were delivered and freed from the slave bondage of Egypt. They were now resting in the wilderness, being fed and protected by God. They were only about a two-week trip away from their promised land, the land of Canaan. This is the same land that God promised

Abraham when He asked Abraham to leave his father's house.

> *Genesis 12:5-7 And Abram took Sarai his wife, and Lot his brother's son, and all their substance that they had gathered, and the souls that they had gotten in Haran; and they went forth to go into the land of Canaan; and into the land of Canaan they came.*
>
> *⁶ And Abram passed through the land unto the place of Sichem, unto the plain of Moreh. And the Canaanite was then in the land.*
>
> *⁷ And the LORD appeared unto Abram, and said, Unto thy seed will I give this land: and there builded he an altar unto the LORD, who appeared unto him.*

Abraham did his part to claim the promise that God showed him would be for his future generation. In verse 7, we see he built an altar to the Lord in that place. Now, hundreds of years later, God is finally leading Abraham's seed into their promised land. However, instead of seeing themselves as God saw them - like lions able to take down giants - they saw themselves as little grasshoppers because that is the "word" they agreed with about themselves. They assumed that was also how their enemy perceived them, although no evidence backed those thoughts.

When you speak negative words, you weaken your identity, you change the atmosphere around you, and you give the spirit of fear entrance into your life. So what happened after these spies, these representatives of the people, explained that the Israelites were grasshoppers compared to the giants of the land? Let's read on.

> *Numbers 14:1- 4 And all the congregation lifted up their voice, and cried; and the people wept that night.*
>
> *2 And all the children of Israel murmured against Moses and against Aaron: and the whole congregation said unto them, Would God that we had died in the land of Egypt! Or would God we had died in this wilderness!*
>
> *3 And wherefore hath the LORD brought us unto this land, to fall by the sword, that our wives and our children should be a prey? Were it not better for us to return into Egypt?*
>
> *4 And they said one to another, Let us make a captain, and let us return into Egypt.*

Here's what came in as a result of this wicked report from the fearful spies. Sorrow filled the camp, the people started to weep, and they murmured and complained against the leadership that had gotten them that far. They had to blame someone for the position they now found themselves in. Then the Israelites decided that the direction they should go was backwards. The people decided that they would pick a leader from among them and go back to Egypt, the place of bondage from which they had been miraculously delivered. One moment of hearing that they were weak led them to make a series of decisions that caused them to live the rest of their days in the wilderness. It averaged to about forty people dying per day for forty years.

All of this could have been avoided if they had listened to the faith of Joshua and Caleb instead of the fearful among them. Joshua and Caleb were two of the twelve spies who were not fearful and did not see themselves as grasshoppers but as fierce, bold lions. They were ready to take care of the opposition and possess the land, just like a lion conquers its prey.

> *Numbers 14:6-9 And Joshua the son of Nun, and Caleb the son of Jephunneh, which were of them that searched the land, rent their clothes:*

7 And they spake unto all the company of the children of Israel, saying, The land, which we passed through to search it, is an exceeding good land.

8 If the LORD delight in us, then he will bring us into this land, and give it us; a land which floweth with milk and honey.

9 Only rebel not ye against the LORD, neither fear ye the people of the land; for they are bread for us: their defence is departed from them, and the LORD is with us: fear them not.

Joshua and Caleb brought a good report of how great the land was and how defenseless the people were in that moment. They encouraged the people to not accept fear. They wanted the people to stop allowing fear to have a place in their hearts and the camp. However, instead of listening and agreeing with these two fearless men, the people wanted to stone them. They wanted to punish the fearless among them for even suggesting that they were winners and well able to do anything this big. Fear wants to prevent you from winning, but you can defeat it.

Numbers 14:10 But all the congregation bade stone them with stones. And the glory of the

LORD *appeared in the tabernacle of the congregation before all the children of Israel.*

Look at how God responded to the fearful multitude coming against the fearless two. We should pay close attention to His response.

Numbers 14:11 And the LORD said unto Moses, How long will this people provoke me? and how long will it be ere they believe me, for all the signs which I have shewed among them?

They created an atmosphere of fear, and the Lord regarded their response of a fearful atmosphere to be a provocation to Him. Here you must stop and examine your own life. Are you creating an atmosphere around you of provocation to God? Are you repeatedly expressing how much you are a nobody, unable to follow God's instructions to occupy a certain territory or anything else He asks of you? Fear will cause you to lose out on the benefits of your freedom that God has given to you. None of these murmurers, complainers, and self-proclaimed grasshoppers got to enter the promised land. Instead, only their children were able to go in, led by the two fearless ones, Joshua and Caleb. The Lord pointed out that Caleb had a different spirit from the complainers and murmurers.

> *Numbers 14:24 But my servant Caleb, because he had another spirit with him, and hath followed me fully, him will I bring into the land whereinto he went; and his seed shall possess it.*

Joshua and Caleb endured fearlessly for forty years while their peers died off. These two men got the reward of speaking faith not fear. They believed it was possible to possess the land while the rest of the camp was ready to stone them.

When you are fearless, you do not go against the plans of God by giving into the negative, fearful decisions of those around you. You will always stand up for God's promises to you and your generations to come. Caleb and Joshua were good men and were able to secure an inheritance for their children's children. According to the Bible, that's what a good man does.

> *Proverbs 13:22 A good man leaveth an inheritance to his children's children. . ."*

Fearlessness causes you to leave a generational surplus. You were created to be fearless. Now go walk in it!

Fearless Actions

These actions can dramatically help you break away from an environment that might not be conducive to your life.

1. What are some words you've heard from family members or friends telling you that you were unable to accomplish what you knew you were called to do? _____

_____

_____

_____

_____

2. What can you do to change the effects of those words now? _____

_____

_____

_____

3. Do you feel guilty about confronting someone or ignoring their advice to you, especially if you consider them a mentor or someone whose opinion you value? _____

_____

_____

Meditation

If you find yourself struggling with guilt feelings to confront or stop a family tradition or words that hold you back, then take some extra time and really mediate on the scriptures below. You need to ask the Holy Spirit to give you a revelation of the difference between loyalty and control.

You can say no to people who want to help you, but lack godly wisdom. You can choose to still be connected to them, without making them a counselor to your future.

- Jeremiah 1:8 Be not afraid of them [their faces], for I am with you to deliver you, says the Lord.

- Psalm 1:2-3 Blessed is the man that walketh not in the counsel of the ungodly, nor standeth in the way of sinners, nor sitteth in the seat of the scornful.

  2 But his delight is in the law of the LORD; and in his law doth he meditate day and night.

  3 And he shall be like a tree planted by the rivers of water, that bringeth forth his fruit in his season; his leaf also shall not wither; and whatsoever he doeth shall prosper.

Chapter Six

The Fearless are Decisive

"Your decisions are based on who you think you are."
– Fiona Pyszka
*"There is no wisdom, no insight, no **plan** that can succeed against the Lord." -* **Proverbs 21:30**

Freedom is a word that is used often in our society today. Even if a person does not feel as free as they would like, they still dream of what their freedom would look like. No one ever sits alone or lies in bed dreaming of how awesome it would be to be imprisoned or in bondage to some sort of an addiction. Everyone dreams of being free from habits, people, responsibilities or something else that they feel restricted in.

Is freedom a good desire or a bad one? Let's take a look at what the Bible says about freedom.

> *Galatians 4:30-31 But what does the Scripture say? Cast out and send away the slave woman and her son, for never shall the son of the slave woman be heir and share the inheritance with the son of the free woman.*

[31] So, brethren, we [who are born again] are not children of a slave woman [the natural], but of the free [the supernatural].

Galatians 5:1 In [this] freedom Christ has made us free [and completely liberated us]; stand fast then, and do not be hampered and held ensnared and submit again to a yoke of slavery [which you have once put off].

We see that the slave woman and her son were to be cast out because the inheritance was never going to be his. This verse is talking about the difference between Hagar's son and Sarah's son, both fathered by Abraham. One son, Ishmael, represents the flesh and the man-made solutions to a problem. The other son, Isaac, represents the Spirit and God's promises to solve problems. Once God's promises are accepted and initiated, the fleshly solutions must be sent packing.

Today our society would put this action in the category of not loving someone. But the bigger picture here is the separation of light and darkness, the promised and the permitted. We have to make decisions for our own life to determine what the future will be. When the natural threatens the supernatural you must let the natural go. The two cannot live together. Both of them carry a yoke. You can't wear two yokes that are going in different directions. Jesus describes the yoke from Him and His kingdom as such.

> *Matthew 11:30 For My yoke is wholesome (useful, good—not harsh, hard, sharp, or pressing, but comfortable, gracious, and pleasant), and My burden is light and easy to be borne.*

There are no words in Jesus' description of His yoke that sounds like a bondage experience. If you're experiencing a pressing, poking, sharpness and manipulative control of your life, you are probably yoked with a fleshly yoke that is trying to prevent you from receiving your inheritance from the Father. Your inheritance is what the Bible says you can have as a believer and child of God. Part of your inheritance comes with the stipulations, as we see in Galatians 4:30-31, that you must put away slavery and a slave mentality (represented by the slave woman) in order to possess your inheritance. Your inheritance includes freedom because God wants you free indeed.

According to Galatians 5:1, we see also it is our responsibility to stand firm and not yield again to slavery. Slavery will attempt to enslave you through fear and the fleshly yoke if it can. It will knock on your door and beg you to let it in. It is a craving that will show up to persuade you to go back to the addiction and take the easier way out by not doing what you were called to do. It may give you alternatives to living a life with people around you, one that keeps you locked behind your walls of man-made protection. **DON'T FALL PREY** to these lies. They are marketing campaigns by your enemy to put you back in bondage. Don't be taken hostage. But what if you did yield again and are currently in bondage? Then you must muster up the strength and courage to decide to be free and stick with that decision until freedom occurs.

The fearless are decisive. They say "yes" or "no" without reservation. They know what they want and they say what they want. This is an important part of being fearless. If you keep wavering between two decisions, according to the Bible nothing will happen. James says it best:

James 1:5-8 If any of you is deficient in wisdom, let him ask of the giving God [Who gives] to everyone liberally and ungrudgingly, without reproaching or faultfinding, and it will be given him.

6 Only it must be in faith that he asks with no wavering (no hesitating, no doubting). For the one who wavers (hesitates, doubts) is like the billowing surge out at sea that is blown hither and thither and tossed by the wind.

7 For truly, let not such a person imagine that he will receive anything [he asks for] from the Lord,

8 [For being as he is] a man of two minds (hesitating, dubious, irresolute), [he is] unstable and unreliable and uncertain about everything [he thinks, feels, decides].

When you begin the journey of second guessing the decisions you make in life, you become prey for the enemy. He knows that if he presents a good enough argument for you to choose him, then he's got you doubting what God says. That's all he wants to do. He doesn't even care if you do what he says; he just wants you to doubt what God says. Then he knows he has a way in. When Satan tempted Eve, he cast doubt on what she knew God said.

Genesis 3:1 Now the serpent was more subtle and crafty than any living creature of the field which the Lord God had made. And he [Satan] said to the woman, Can it really be that God has said, You shall not eat from every tree of the garden?

That started the downward spiral cycle of mankind. Eve accepted the lie and then influenced Adam to make a decision based on Satan's doubt seed in her heart about what God said.

Today we can learn from the story of Adam and Eve so we don't repeat their mistakes. You see the picture of what devastation indecisive doubt can bring. You now know how to defeat the enemy that wants to put you in slavery. You must give him a decisive "no," and you must give God a decisive "yes."

God's anointing and power is strong and able to deliver and release you from any bondage that the enemy dares to snare you in. Even if you've given a "yes" to bondage again, or never said "no" to begin with, you can do so now. Bondage does not have to take a grip on you. The bars of slavery are opened by the master key named Jesus. He holds all the keys and can open any door. You just say the name of Jesus now. Ask Jesus to release you from bondage, surrender to His yoke, and ask Him to take you on your journey in life. Ask Him now and He will do it. His anointing was given to make you slippery to bondage so it can't get a grip on you. You can slide right out of those chains. Here's how Isaiah said it:

> Isaiah 10:27 And it shall come to pass in that day, that his burden shall be taken away from off thy shoulder, and his yoke from off thy neck, and the yoke shall be destroyed because of the anointing.

This scripture shows us that the anointing of God is capable of breaking you out of yokes of slavery. You were created to be free through Jesus Christ. Don't fear the enemy that wants to keep you bound.

Many people stay bound because they are held hostage to someone's provision, attention, or even relationship with their children. The threat is held over them, "If you leave or if you defy me I will do this or that to you or your children or family." If you say "yes" to Jesus' yoke He covers you and protects you, and He will lead you out of bondage as He planned. He will also provide you with what you need so you don't have to rely on another master. His plans are activated through faith in believing what He said. He told you already that if you take His yoke and burden, it will be easier and lighter for you. You MUST believe this to live a fearless life. You cannot live a fearless life believing the lie that a human was designed to provide for your needs.

If you've read this far, I know you are serious about being fearless. Be sure to stabilize your knowledge on the subject of freedom. Study it in the Bible and get books that could help you further. You must understand the depth of freedom you have in Jesus. Use your faith in Jesus to overcome the world.

> *1 John 5:4 For whatsoever is born of God overcometh the world: and this is the victory that overcometh the world, even our faith.*

You will see how faith overcomes fear in the next chapter. You faith is an effective tool to disarm the Spirit of fear.

Fearless Actions

1. What do you see now in your life that is a yoke that does not come from God? _____

_____

_____

_____

2. Why have you kept it there? _____

_____

_____

3. After reading this chapter, write down the actions you will now take to resist and breakaway from this yoke of slavery? (Do not skip this part) _____

_____

_____

4. Write down today's date, and make a decisive statement in writing that from this day forth you give the Holy Spirit permission to arrest your thoughts and actions, should you choose to go to that bondage again. _____

_____

_____

Meditation

Meditate on these scriptures to assist in renewing your mind to your new-found liberty. You must do this part so that the area that was once held in bondage is now replaced with new information that supports your freedom.

- Luke 4:18 "The Spirit of the Lord is on me, because he has anointed me to proclaim good news to the poor. He has sent me to proclaim freedom for the prisoners and recovery of sight for the blind, to set the oppressed free,
- 2 Corinthians 3:17 Now the Lord is that Spirit: and where the Spirit of the Lord is, there is liberty.
- Galatians 5:1 Stand fast therefore in the liberty wherewith Christ hath made us free, and be not entangled again with the yoke of bondage.
- Galatians 5:13 For you, brethren, were [indeed] called to freedom; only [do not let your] freedom be an incentive to your flesh and an opportunity or excuse [for selfishness], but through love you should serve one another.
- 2 Peter 2:19 They promise them liberty, when they themselves are the slaves of depravity and defilement—for by whatever anyone is made inferior or worse or is overcome, to that [person or thing] he is enslaved.
- Psalm 119:45 And I will walk at liberty and at ease, for I have sought and inquired for [and desperately required] Your precepts.

Chapter Seven
The Currency of the Fearless

"Your identity should not change because of your circumstances." - **Fiona Pyszka**
"So then faith cometh by hearing, and hearing by the word of God." - **Romans 10:17**

It was a hot July afternoon, a little after noon, when I heard someone panting heavily as they tried to say "hello" in our church sanctuary. I was in my office in the church. I stepped out in the dark auditorium to see a police officer trying to catch his breath. It was obvious he had been running or on a long walk. At this moment many thoughts were running through my mind, including, "I wonder what he needs because Doug (my husband) is not here and most likely I'll have to ask him to wait or get back to him." I didn't realize that he was there to give me information about Doug.

The officer proceeded to ask me if I knew of someone driving a green car. I replied that I did, as it was the color of our car, the car my husband and son just left in. He then said that there had been an accident and he needed me to come with him. He indicated to me that Doug was no longer unconscious and he was happy to tell me that. Immediately, I heard in my spirit, "Doug is indestructible because he is faith man." Since indestructible is not a word that I use in my everyday language, I knew it had come into my spirit from the Spirit of God. I knew it was a rhema word for that moment in time. So I went with that word in my heart, as I made my way with the officer to the place of the accident. I told my mind and agreed with my spirit that no matter what I was about to see, Doug was faith man, and he was indestructible. All this time I thought there was a car accident, so I asked the officer if my son was okay. He indicated that he was okay so they left him in the car so they could work on his dad. I was puzzled by the answer, as I thought, "If the car was wrecked then why would they leave my son in it?" My answer became more apparent as we went outside.

There is a long driveway that leads to the road in front of our church property, so even though I could see the big things, I couldn't see the little details of what was happening. What I saw was two fire trucks, three to five police cars, an ambulance and quite a few busy people on the scene. I saw our green car at the end of the church driveway, and I asked the officer, "How was the car hit?"

He said, "Oh, it wasn't the car that was hit, it was your husband. He was hit as a pedestrian."

That's when it all made sense -- the words of the police, the words in my spirit, and the need to know that Doug was indestructible because of faith. I needed to know that before I saw what I was about to see.

I saw was my young son (about 3 or 4 at the time) in the back of the car with the windows up and his face blood-red from the heat. I immediately opened the car door to get him out. He was calm and said that he didn't come out of the car even when he saw daddy was hit because he knew God would take care of daddy. If my son had run out on the road after his dad, he could have gotten hit himself as it was a busy intersection. That was miracle number one.

I then went to Doug who was lying on a stretcher, strapped in with EMTs watching over him about to hoist him into the ambulance. I stopped them to ask him if he was okay. All the while there was blood running on the road from his face, It looked like blood was pouring from his ears. So what do you do in those moments? That's when you'd better believe that the faith in God you have is real.

I knew that the words and the atmosphere around Doug from the moment everyone got on the scene was one of anxiousness and fear. I knew that on the way there the EMTs might have been discussing how much trauma there might have been as it was a pedestrian head-on collision with a big van. I had to change the atmosphere with my faith words, so I proceeded to say, "Father, in Jesus' Name I declare that Doug is whole, there are no broken bones and no side effects in this body. He is 100% whole and healed in Jesus' name."

Well, you can imagine the stares and looks of "this poor lady, she is just in shock," that I got. All I needed was to know that God was there, real, and able to deliver. Doug agreed with me and off he went into the ambulance. Miracle number two.

Exactly twenty-four hours after the time of the accident, Doug walked out of the hospital on his own. No broken bones, no side effects, and no head injuries. He had bruises and stiff muscles, but he was not traumatized. Our finances were not even affected at all even though we did not have medical insurance because the medical part of our car insurance took care of the over $25,000 hospital bill. Miracle number three.

I tell you this story because it was real to our family and we saw real results. Today, Doug is preaching the gospel as he was destined to and our son is not traumatized by the events of that day. Instead, our son knows that God protects us as we are His children. He knows that there is nothing God can't do if we will only believe when we ask.

> Romans 10:17 So then faith cometh by hearing, and hearing by the word of God.

We see here that faith comes. It's not just pushed on us. Faith comes by hearing God's Word. When hearing is enacted, then the faith of what we are hearing comes. It takes faith to believe what God promised us and speaks to us is true and real. We have to develop and build our faith everyday so when things happen in life we are prepared. We shouldn't have to try to do it in the moment of the event. Now, if you're already in a situation, by all means, build your faith even while you're going through, God will see you till the end. Don't wait for something to happen; build faith in God now.

> *Mark 11:22 "Have faith in God," Jesus answered.*

Jesus told us to have faith in God. God is the source of life we should all be hooked into. He is the Spirit to which our spirits should be feeding. However, Satan is God's adversary and he wants God's Kingdom, God's power, and the worship that God alone receives. The only way he can do this is by giving you another spirit to hook up with -- the spirit of fear. Satan uses fear to gain entrance into people's lives. After all, fear is faith in the devil.

If I had hooked up with fear when I heard the news of Doug's accident, there would have been a very different result to the story of his accident. I believe that if there were broken bones in his body or trauma to his head, it was all fixed because I said on earth what God declared in heaven. That's what Jesus' model prayer to his disciples said should happen. He taught them to declare on earth as it is in heaven.

> *Matthew 6:10 Thy kingdom come, Thy will be done in earth, as it is in heaven.*

It is our responsibility to work faith. We work it out through confession, believing, and then expecting to see results. Faith comes by hearing. So what we hear is important and influences what we believe. Some things require immediate results while others require timing. The spirit of fear comes in to stop your faith from having its full maturity in a matter. The only ingredient needed for faith to not mature in a matter is fear. Why? Because fear brings distrust and unbelief towards God. Fear makes you look at God with questions concerning His Word. Fear gives you comparison analysis to consider, and it causes you to look at past failures and relationships and compare how those turned out to how it will turn out with God. You must stop and tell fear and fear's master, Satan, that, "God is not a man. God does not compare to man. God is God and there is none like Him and there never will be."

God is the highest authority in which you can believe. If He says anything then that is the last word on the matter. Period! You must get this into your spirit. You must renew your mind to this element of faith in God. This is a life or death truth that will determine whether you live a life of "what-ifs" or a life of "it is." It is because God said it is.

> Romans 3:3 What if some did not believe and were without faith? Does their lack of faith and their faithlessness nullify and make ineffective and void the faithfulness of God and His fidelity [to His Word]?
>
> 4 By no means! Let God be found true though every human being is false and a liar, as it is written, That You may be justified and shown to be upright in what You say, and prevail when You are judged [by sinful men].

You can never nullify the word of God or decrease its value. However, you can prevent it from operating in your own life. So be careful about putting God's Word in the same category as the word of other relationships in your life. God's Word is far greater, much more powerful, and will always be true. Whether you believe it or not is up to you, but the potency and value of it is not changed by your opinion of it.

Many people view God as they do their earthy father. This could be a big error. No matter how great your earthly father is, the Bible calls them evil when compared to God. Take a look.

> Matthew 7:8-11 For every one that asketh receiveth; and he that seeketh findeth; and to him that knocketh it shall be opened.
>
> 9 Or what man is there of you, whom if his son ask bread, will he give him a stone?
>
> 10 Or if he ask a fish, will he give him a serpent?
>
> 11 If ye then, being evil, know how to give good gifts unto your children, how much more shall your Father which is in heaven give good things to them that ask him?

I believe that because of this passage many people compare God to their own father. But what is being shown here is that there is no comparison. The fathers on earth are considered evil to our Father in heaven. Even the ones that would give the food that the children request are still considered evil compared to God. To be fearless you must stop all comparisons between God and the relationships you have on this earth. As great as they may be, they have no power to bless you like God can. Even the fatherly blessings here on earth are hooked in with the heavenly Father's power. God created you and He has the ability to pull out of you supernatural abilities, purposes, and dreams that can make you the head and not the tail, make you above and not beneath. These are things that your earthly father does not have the power to do.

So this is where you can release yourself from the fear of being rejected by God like you were rejected in important relationships in your life. If that relationship was a father, mother, husband, wife, or close friend, they are not God, and they don't hold the keys to your future. Only God does. This knowledge alone will give you confidence to walk in faith after God's heart. Here is what God said about Himself.

> Revelation 1:8 I am Alpha and Omega, the beginning and the ending, saith the Lord, which is, and which was, and which is to come, the Almighty.

God is already where you're trying to go in the future. Imagine that for a moment. God is the beginning and end. That means that God didn't start His life the same time we did, and He's not ending it on earth when ours ends. He's already been in the past, is currently in the present and is waiting for us in the future. Can you make that statement about anyone else in your life? Absolutely not! No one else knows what's going to happen tomorrow, let alone your future. Only God does. So when the spirit of fear comes to intimidate you and tell you what your future looks like, you must say out loud, "That is a lie, only God knows my future, and I believe and trust Him." Say it out loud now, just for practice.

God's tomorrow for you is already written. It was written before you were born. The question is, will you choose God's choices for you or fear's prediction of what you future will be? Whatever you choose is what you walk in. But here is what God says about your future.

> *Psalm 139:16 Your eyes saw my unformed substance, and in Your book all the days [of my life] were written before ever they took shape, when as yet there was none of them.*

Does this mean that there is a hard-coded book written about you and, no matter what, that's what will happen? No, it means that God has a perfect plan, but you get to choose between it or a permissive plan for your life. The permissive plan is the one that we follow when we override God's leading and suggestions by our own way and will. We all have a will and God respects it. He proved it when He did not stop Adam and Eve from sinning. He proves it every day as people sin and participate in evil. Yet, if people will call on God from earth, He will hear from heaven and send instructions to His people who will listen to cause a change in our nations, communities and homes. He said it best here,

> 2 Chronicles 7:14 If my people, which are called by my name, shall humble themselves, and pray, and seek my face, and turn from their wicked ways; then will I hear from heaven, and will forgive their sin, and will heal their land.

When we read this verse, we should not just think about our land as the immediate place or country that we live in. We should consider our land the entire earth. God wants people on earth to take responsibility to pray on earth what He has declared in heaven. He wants us to call heaven on earth. But sometimes people are too afraid to do something for their own land, let alone do something for the whole earth. When God set Adam and Eve in the Garden of Eden, He commanded them to subdue the earth.

> Genesis 1:28 God blessed them and said to them, "Be fruitful and increase in number; fill the

earth and subdue it. Rule over the fish in the sea and the birds in the sky and over every living creature that moves on the ground."

God's instruction for Adam and Eve was not just for the Garden of Eden but for them to take the model of the Garden to the whole earth. That's what we are supposed to do with our own life. Take the model of what God has given us into our towns, communities, and countries, and take it to the world. We take it through our words first then our actions.

God spoke into existence everything that manifested in the natural. He spoke order to this formless earth into existence, and He spoke Jesus' appearance on earth before He ever came. So we should model our life after God's example of building something from nothing or repairing something that's broken.

What does all of this have to do with faith? It has everything to do with faith. If we can't believe what God did as the ultimate model of how to do things now, then we will always be searching for new ways to do things. That's when the spirit of fear can present its proposal to cause you to be sidetracked and go for a plan that was never intended for you as a child of God.

The currency of the fearless is faith. Faith gives your words value. If you mix any amount of fear with your words you change the value of your words. You become an unstable investment. People will not feel confident agreeing with you because you are not confident of what you're speaking. How then could someone else vouch for your words that you are not in agreement with.

I love the way Reinhard Bonnke puts this in his most recent facebook post[3]:

> "When we do business with people, we need money. When we do business with God, we need faith. Faith is the currency in the Kingdom of God." REINHARD BONNKE

We cannot do transactions on earth for God without the currency of faith. Faith is absolutely necessary and fear is the debt that eats up your faith. Don't be in debt to fear and to Satan. Jesus' blood and His sacrifice has already paid the debt you owed for sin. You don't owe Satan anything else. You now

---

[3] http://www.facebook.com/evangelistreinhardbonnke

owe it to God to dismiss Satan's lies from your presence and from your life.

Increase the value of your faith words today. Believe God, hear His Word and speak His word continually in your world. That's how you build strong faith and give fear the boot. Kick fear out just like God kicked Satan out of heaven (see Luke 10:18).

Fearless Actions

1. Do you feel as though your faith currency has a high value right now? _____

   _____

   _____

   _____

2. What recent transactions have you made to give an example of the value of your faith currency (i.e. an area in your life you have used faith recently)? Did your currency work or not? _____

   _____

   _____

3. What do you believe is the reason for the results you received? _____

   _____

_____

_____

_____

4. Is there anything you need to do differently to increase the value of your faith? If so, what? _

_____

Meditation

Here are some faith words to help build your mind up as you grow your faith currency. When you meditate on these verses, make them personal. Put your name in places or say "I."

- Romans 10:17 So then faith cometh by hearing, and hearing by the word of God.
- Mark 4:9 Then Jesus said, "Whoever has ears to hear, let them hear."
- Romans 1:8 First, I thank my God through Jesus Christ for you all, that your faith is spoken of throughout the whole world.
- Romans 1:17 For therein is the righteousness of God revealed from faith to faith: as it is written, The just shall live by faith.

- Romans 4:20 He staggered not at the promise of God through unbelief; but was strong in faith, giving glory to God;
- Romans 5:1 Therefore being justified by faith, we have peace with God through our Lord Jesus Christ:
- 1 Corinthians 2:5 That your faith should not stand in the wisdom of men, but in the power of God.

Chapter Eight
The Mind of the Fearless

"Your mind has the ability to change just by the exercising of your will." - **Fiona Pyszka**

"Wherefore gird up the loins of your mind, be sober, and hope to the end for the grace that is to be brought unto you at the revelation of Jesus Christ." - **1 Peter 1:13**

In scripture, we see the transformation story of a man named Saul who later became Paul. This man was not good news to Christians. He had a reputation of persecuting, imprisoning, and killing Christians. He was the one who would take Christians to prison just because they believed in Jesus. He was also the man that held the cloaks of those who stoned Stephen and killed him. Yet this man who exerted such fear into people became a leader for Christianity. He had a dramatic transformation and became the writer for many of the books of the New Testament.

One of the traits I admire about Paul is the total transformation of his mind. He truly demonstrated what it looks like to become a new creation in Christ

Jesus. He showed us what it looks like for the old to pass away and for all things to become new.

Paul would have had every right to keep having nightmares about his past. He could relive the time that he stood there while Stephen was stoned, or remember the faces of the families of those he had taken to prison for being a Christian. Instead we see him walking in the provision of what God did for him through Jesus Christ. And he did this guilt-free.

Paul is a beautiful example of a person who lived a guilt-free life as a Christian, no matter how bad of a sinner he was before. He understood that a Christian becomes a brand new creation in Christ. Being a new creation means that you never before existed, so remembering the past that linked you to the sinner you were is irrelevant because technically your old man is dead.

Paul comprehended all of this. I believe it was this understanding in Paul's mind that gave him the ability to be fearless. He was put in so many situations that caused him to face life-and-death situations, yet he never once acted in fear. Instead he was fearless and did many miracles, signs, and wonders.

There is a certain mindset that is common in the fearless. They are bold and fierce yet humble and always learning. What was Paul's secret to being so fearless? I believe he said it best in his message to the Romans:

> *Romans 12:2 And be not conformed to this world: but be ye transformed by the renewing of your mind, that ye may prove what is that good, and acceptable, and perfect, will of God.*

He then gave another charge to the Ephesian church.

> *Ephesians 4:23 And be renewed in the spirit of your mind.*

There is something about a renewed mind that frees you from being stuck in the past. It's the past habits and people that can cause the spirit of fear to enter a situation and give you results that were once given before. The spirit of fear will never show you a winning result, but it will always emphasize your points of failure. That's why fear has been so effective in working on those who have forgotten to renew their mind. This is a daily exercise. You should daily pray and ask the Holy Spirit to teach you something new. The information you had yesterday may need to be updated today to represent what God is doing now in this season. When we walk in a sound mind, fear is afraid of us. We see this in the example of David and King Saul. Every time David would operate in the anointing Saul would get afraid and try to kill him (see 1 Samuel 16:11-23 and 1 Samuel 18:7-17).

God had chosen David to be king instead of Saul. Saul was not humble enough to keep God's instructions or to let someone else get praised more than him, so he developed pride. Saul's pride increased so much that he felt threatened by David and sought to kill him for no reason. How did David defend himself and still stay true to God? David did not get to take the throne for years after he was anointed king. Instead of forging for himself the path to kingship, he waited on God's timing and instruction. He protected himself by fleeing Saul's presence, and he walked with and waited on God.

One way that you can keep hope alive and continue waiting for what God promised you without fear is to know that God has placed you on this earth because He wanted you here. You must know that God purposefully created you for this time in history. I love how the Message Bible says this:

Revelation 4:11 Worthy, O Master! Yes, our
God! Take the glory! the honor! the power! You
created it all; It was created because you
wanted it.

We see the elders and the creatures in heaven agreeing that God gets the glory, honor, and power for everything. They also note that God created them all and that He did it because He wanted to. It was God's choice for you to be here on earth -- not your parents, not society, but God.

You must renew your mind to this fact now. You have to believe and accept that God planned your life even before anyone else knew you. You are that special. We all are. You must believe this truth. Renew your mind to this truth now. Here's how He said it to Jeremiah.

Jeremiah 1:5 Before I formed you in the womb I
knew [and] approved of you [as My chosen
instrument], and before you were born I
separated and set you apart, consecrating you;
[and] I appointed you as a prophet to the
nations.

Put yourself in this verse; see God speaking to you. You may not be called as a prophet to the nations, but if you know what you've been called to, then put that in the verse too. Take charge of speaking on earth what God says and thinks about you. He is not secretive of His thoughts or words about you. Ask Him and He will tell you. You don't get answers in life because you simply don't ask or you ask the wrong questions. In my book, "The Purpose of You," I share how you can know and follow your purpose. I believe that everyone was created with a purpose for their specific time and season on the earth. You were created for this time and for a specific reason; now renew your mind to that.

Why is this so important in being fearless? It is important because when you know your purpose and who God created you to be, fear cannot steal it from you. You must be confident and convinced of this truth. Your mind must reflect your knowledge. This will cause it to be settled in your heart, and what is settled in your heart will come out of your mouth. If you do not know, you cannot speak with assurance, and what you cannot say with assurance, your mind and body will interpret as a lie.

Don't deceive yourself; be fully persuaded in your mind of who you are and who God is to you. Abraham was fully persuaded that God would fulfill what He had promised: that Abraham was truly going to be the father of many nations. We see in Romans how persuaded Abraham was:

> *Romans 4:21 And being fully persuaded that, what he had promised, he was able also to perform.*

God does not lie, whatever He says comes to pass. You must renew your mind that God is not incapable of bringing His Words to pass.

> *Numbers 23:19 God is not a man, that he should lie; neither the son of man, that he should repent: hath he said, and shall he not do it? or hath he spoken, and shall he not make it good?*

So what should you do now to be fearless? You must renew your mind to the possibilities of God, not the obstacles of fear. Remember, fear is a spirit that wants to take over your mind, but God is a Spirit that wants to renew your mind.

Fearless Actions

1. What thoughts come to you most often to cause you to fear the future? _____

_____

_____

_____

2. Do you ever find yourself thinking that you are just not good enough to do anything of significance? _____

_____

_____

3. Now that you've identified these two areas (in questions 1 and 2) write down new actions you will take to eliminate these thoughts and start believing God's Words about you: _____

_____

_____

_____

_____

Meditation

Take time now to meditate on these scriptures to renew your mind.

- Isaiah 40:31 But they that wait upon the Lord shall renew their strength; they shall mount up with wings as eagles; they shall run, and not be weary; and they shall walk, and not faint.

- Psalm 59:9 Because of his strength will I wait upon thee: for God is my defense.
- Luke 12:32 Fear not, little flock; for it is your Father's good pleasure to give you the kingdom.
- 1 Corinthians 2:16 for, "Who has known the mind of the Lord so as to instruct him?" But we have the mind of Christ.
- Isaiah 26:3 Thou wilt keep him in perfect peace, whose mind is stayed on thee: because he trusteth in thee.

Chapter Nine
The Triple Threat

"Become the biggest nightmare for evil, let fear run when it sees you coming." - **Fiona Pyszka**
"The fear of man bringeth a snare: but whoso putteth his trust in the Lord shall be safe." – **Proverbs 29:25**

Let's take a look again at the verse in 2 Timothy.

> *2 Timothy 1:7 For God hath not given us the spirit of fear; but of power, and of love, and of a sound mind.*

We see in this verse that fear is identified as a spirit. More importantly, power, love and a sound mind are all from God's Spirit. These three representations of the Spirit of God combine to form the triple threat you must use against the spirit of fear. God and Satan are not equal foes. They don't match up in power and authority. Satan is a created being and he has no power over God. That was demonstrated once and for all when God fired him from heaven.

Ezekiel 28:15 Thou wast perfect in thy ways from the day that thou wast created, till iniquity was found in thee.

Luke 10:18 And He said to them, I saw Satan falling like a lightning [flash] from heaven.

Satan has an agenda to intimidate God's children and His creation into worshiping Satan instead of Almighty God. Our responsibility as Christians is to know what Spirit we are of so that we can tap into the power available to us through the Holy Spirit. Here are some verses that explain the Spirit of power.

Luke 1:35 The angel answered, "The Holy Spirit will come on you, and the power of the Most High will overshadow you. So the holy one to be born will be called the Son of God.

We see here how God came and dwelt among us in the form of Jesus: the Holy Spirit's power had to overshadow Mary. It was the power of the Holy Spirit that was implanted in her, and this power caused her to carry Jesus to full term, the Word. Jesus was born because of the power of the Spirit of God that overshadowed Mary.

The Spirit of power is the first part of the triple threat against the spirit of fear. The Spirit of power enabled the Word to be planted, to grow, and to mature. Jesus is the Word made flesh.

> *John 1:14 The Word became flesh and made his dwelling among us. We have seen his glory, the glory of the one and only Son, who came from the Father, full of grace and truth.*

The Holy Spirit came in power on the day of Pentecost as the people waited in the upper room. They were told that when the Holy Spirit came on them they would receive power to be witnesses.

> *Acts 1:8 But you shall receive power (ability, efficiency, and might) when the Holy Spirit has come upon you, and you shall be My witnesses in Jerusalem and all Judea and Samaria and to the ends (the very bounds) of the earth.*
>
> *Acts 2:4 And they were all filled with the Holy Ghost, and began to speak with other tongues, as the Spirit gave them utterance.*

Sure enough, after the Holy Spirit came on them, they all went out and were witnesses to the people visiting the town. They went out in power. They had power to speak of something that changed the lives of the people. When they spoke, they didn't even know the language they were speaking.

Acts 2:7-8 And they were all amazed and marvelled, saying one to another, Behold, are not all these which speak Galilaeans?

8 And how hear we every man in our own tongue, wherein we were born?

The Spirit of power allows you to speak things that are needed when they are needed. One of the tactics of the spirit of fear is to manipulate and intimidate with words. This spirit manipulates you through reasoning and the illusion to make you think it knows more than it does. All of the information from the spirit of fear is a lie. Although it may start with some truth to get you hooked into listening, that truth is perverted and twisted into a lie.

The Spirit of power gives you the ability to stand up as a witness for truth. You can stand up and witness to who God is and what God can do. You don't have to listen to fear anymore. If you just realize that the language of fear is lies – twisted, deceiving, controlling lies – you can resist it and stop it from entering your life.

Stand up in the Spirit of power and defend the truth of God in your life. Defend the truth of who God created you to be. Defend the truth of why you are here on this earth. There is a truth about you that the devil wants to pervert with his lies. The spirit of fear is the catalyst Satan uses to embed his lies as a seed in you. Once embedded he then controls everything you do. When you're in church or an anointed environment of God's power you are able to stand up on the inside for what you want to do. For example, you may decide to step out in faith and go to the nations, defend the poor and needy, and rise up to do the things you've dreamt of doing. However, as soon as you leave that environment and go back to your home, you find fear gripping your thoughts: "How is that supposed to happen?" or "You're not qualified to do that." How about this beauty: "You're not smart enough," and the most common of all, "Who do you think you are?"

It's time that you start creating a faith script, which is a set of scriptures and confessions that you meditate on to silence the lies from Satan. Your faith script will include scriptures that tell you who you are because of Christ. These scriptures show you that you are the head and not the tail, above and not beneath (see Deuteronomy 28).

Many people get defeated by fear because people in positions of power use fear to keep others in line. If this is your situation, then there is something you must NEVER EVER forget. Are you ready? There is no one, absolutely no one, on this planet that has been given authority over your will. No one has veto power over what God says you should do and what God created you to do. The only person that created the blueprint for your life and sent you here is God. Therefore, no one else can make you or pull rank on you when it comes to making decisions for your own life.

Now, I know many people are saying, "Well what about husbands and wives? Aren't wives supposed to submit to their husbands? What about children? Aren't they are supposed to obey their parents?" These are good questions, so let's look at some verses that talk about this.

> Ephesians 5:22 Wives, submit yourselves unto your own husbands, as unto the Lord.
>
> Colossians 3:18 Wives, submit yourselves unto your own husbands, as it is fit in the Lord.

We see that in these verses, there is a clause that tells the wife how she should submit, "as unto the

Lord," or "as is fit in the Lord." Just looking at this we see that God has built into the order of the family the clause that He truly is the head of the family, just like He is the head of the church. He is the one who is to be followed. The husband gets to lead according to the charge God gives him. If the husband is going against God's charge, then the wife can refuse to follow her husband if it is not fitting unto the Lord. Many people have misinterpreted this passage for centuries, and this has put many women in the church under such bondage that they have been depressed and oppressed their whole lives.

For some of you, this is a shocking statement to be in the middle of a chapter on the power of God, but let me tell you that it is the power of God that will cause you to stand up for what is right. When a woman agrees with a man because he is her husband and they conspire to do something against God's will, they will both suffer the consequences. There is a way out though: she can disagree or go against her husband's plans. God gives you opportunities to say "no" to evil and "yes" to righteousness.

Here is a story where a husband and wife agreed to do evil even though they had an opportunity to choose the right thing.

> *Acts 5:1-3 But a certain man named Ananias, with Sapphira his wife, sold a possession,[2] And kept back part of the price, his wife also being privy to it, and brought a certain part, and laid it at the apostles' feet.[3] But Peter said, Ananias, why hath Satan filled thine heart to lie to the Holy Ghost, and to keep back part of the price of the land?*
>
> *Acts 5:5 And Ananias hearing these words fell down, and gave up the ghost: and great fear came on all them that heard these things.*

Here we see a man pretending to do something great and honorable for others to see, yet he was acting to deceive and cover up his greed and covetousness. He brought his wife in on it, and she agreed with him. By the power of the Holy Spirit, Peter exposed their attempt to lie. We see that this man did not get an opportunity to repent, and he died immediately after Peter identified his sin.

Then three hours later, in walks his wife.

Acts 5:8-10 And Peter answered unto her, Tell me whether ye sold the land for so much? And she said, Yea, for so much.

⁹ Then Peter said unto her, How is it that ye have agreed together to tempt the Spirit of the Lord? behold, the feet of them which have buried thy husband are at the door, and shall carry thee out.

¹⁰ Then fell she down straightway at his feet, and yielded up the ghost: and the young men came in, and found her dead, and, carrying her forth, buried her by her husband.

When Sapphira walked in, Peter gave her the opportunity to repent. He asked her, "Tell me whether ye sold the land for so much?" This was her safe way out. The Holy Spirit was working through Peter to give her a way out. She refused to disagree with her husband and kept her agreement with him. This caused her to receive the same consequence as her husband, immediate death.

Don't follow the path of someone who purposefully deceives and disobeys the instructions or commands of God. Voice your disapproval, especially when the Holy Spirit gives you an opportunity to expose the lie. Take the safe way out!

Another story that shows different results is the story of Abigail and Nabal in 1 Samuel 25. As you read it you will see that Abigail did not agree with Nabal's disrespect for David and his men. David's recourse for this behavior was to kill Nabal and his entire generation. When Nabal's wife heard of this potential crisis to her family as a result of her husband's harsh words towards God's anointed king, she took action. What did she do? She went against everything her husband said and fed David and his men. She even apologized for her husband's foolish behavior.

For this wise move, what happened to her? She wasn't struck by lightning or punished by God for eternity. Instead here's what happened.

> *1 Samuel 25:39 And when David heard that Nabal was dead, he said, Blessed be the LORD, that hath pleaded the cause of my reproach from the hand of Nabal, and hath kept his servant from evil: for the LORD hath returned the wickedness of Nabal upon his own head. And David sent and communed with Abigail, to take her to him to wife.*

Here's a synopsis. Nabal died, Abigail became the wife of a king, end of story. How do you want your story to end? I just gave you two examples. Ask the Holy Spirit to share with you what you might be afraid of. If God is not the author of the instructions you are agreeing with and following, then take God's way out. Look for it, it's there.

The Spirit of power was given to you to overcome the spirit of fear. Power does not cower at confrontation; it withstands it. Be brave and move forward against the spirit of fear in your life with God's power.

A partner to the Spirit of power is the Spirit of love. The second cord of the triple threat to the spirit of fear is love. It is the ingredient missing from Satan's life. Satan is all fear, and God is all love.

> *1 John 4:18 There is no fear in love; but perfect love casteth out fear: because fear hath torment. He that feareth is not made perfect in love.*

Perfect love comes only from the Spirit of God, therefore the Spirit of love is perfect love. Being in tune with the Holy Spirit means we are tuned in to perfect love. We cannot fight the spirit of fear without the Spirit of love that comes from God. Fear is cast out when perfect love is present. Fear cannot stand the presence of love because fear brings torment and love brings freedom. Torment and freedom are enemies. A person that's free from fear is in the presence of the Spirit of love.

> *Psalm 23:4 Yea, though I walk through the valley of the shadow of death, I will fear no evil: for thou art with me; thy rod and thy staff they comfort me.*

We have to know that fearing evil is to ignore that God is with us. When we get a revelation that God is with us, we will fear no evil. I like what Psalm 91 has to say about evil coming near your dwelling.

> *Psalm 91:10 There shall no evil befall thee, neither shall any plague come nigh thy dwelling.*

We are covered by the protection of Almighty God. We have to get a revelation of this to realize that we are in His trust and care. The spirit of fear is connected to evil, and evil cannot dwell or win in the presence of God.

Love is not the bowing down and handing over of your life for anyone to trample on it, because God's love is strong. The God kind of love is the pursuit of what God would pursue. God pursues those that are searching for Him. Those who have chosen to purposefully reject God do not get the benefit of His love. He loves the world and sent Jesus, but not everyone will benefit from what Jesus did. Why? Because not everyone has received what Jesus did for them personally. God is a God of order, and because He gave man his will, He will not override man's decision. In other words, God will move heaven and earth for people who ask for His help, but He will not move a speck of dust for those who willfully reject His help. Operate in the Spirit of love like God does. You can read in the Bible how God treats His enemies and his friends. God treats them differently. The following is a verse in the Bible on how to express love that often gets misinterpreted:

> Matthew 5:44 But I say unto you, Love your enemies, bless them that curse you, do good to them that hate you, and pray for them which despitefully use you, and persecute you;

If we look closely we will see that the verse says to show love, bless, and do good. It says of those who persecute and despitefully use you that you should pray for them but not let them continue to do those wrong things to you. Many people confuse how to show love and how to fight the good fight of faith. The Bible tells us to do both. So how do we do that?

Fear would love to instruct you on what God means when He says certain phrases, but the spirit of fear does not have the authority to interpret God's Word. The Holy Spirit is the one assigned to interpret God's Word for you.

> *John 16:13 Howbeit when he, the Spirit of truth, is come, he will guide you into all truth: for he shall not speak of himself; but whatsoever he shall hear, that shall he speak: and he will shew you things to come.*

Love is a fruit of the Spirit of God; therefore, only the Holy Spirit should be giving you interpretations of God's Word, not the spirit of fear.

So stop letting fear decide how you love people or what you accept and reject from people around you. The spirit of fear perverts God's love and causes you to tolerate abuse, destruction, and misuse of your gifts and purpose from God.

Don't buy the lie; kick it out of your life. Verbally say right now, "The only spirit I take instructions from is the Holy Spirit." Amen!

The third part of the triple threat is a sound mind. Having a sound mind is a huge advantage in fighting the spirit of fear and evil in general. A sound mind is vital because it gives you clarity in your thoughts so you can answer a matter wisely. It operates in wisdom and understanding.

One of the maneuvers of the spirit of fear is to present a dare, which is a trap to have your ego prove something. When you do things motivated by ego you will also run into pride. The spirit of fear entices you to take a defensive posture, tricking you to defend people you love, even if they are wrong or ungodly. Soon, you will lose sight of fear operating and you could be paralyzing your future and preventing yourself from moving forward.

Fear is a thief and it always wants to rob you of opportunities and promotion. If you stick to your standard and trust God and His agenda for your life, God will promote you because promotion comes from God alone.

> Psalm 75:6-7 For promotion cometh neither from the east, nor from the west, nor from the south.
> 7 But God is the judge: he putteth down one, and setteth up another.

When you know what's available to you from God and that you don't have to toil to get it, you disarm fear's power and leverage over you. Fear will have power over you as long as it has leverage over you. Disarm fear's control by trusting in God and speaking boldly against it with God's words. When you know that God will back you up no matter what, you can become bold in what you say, how you behave, and what you tolerate in your life.

A sound mind is a sober mind. It is a mind ready to participate in orders from Almighty God. You cannot be drunk in your mind if you want to ward off the spirit of fear. To be sober-minded is to think clearly without the manipulations of what-ifs and anxious thoughts of not knowing what to do. A sober mind looks at the truth of who you are in Christ and what you can do through Christ. A sober-minded person bases decisions on this information. Peter says it this way:

> 1 Peter 5:8 Be alert and of sober mind. Your enemy the devil prowls around like a roaring lion looking for someone to devour.

Don't' show up to a fight drunk in your mind. Make sure that your wisdom and understanding is intact.

You are well positioned to hear from God's Spirit about how to respond to your situation. God has given you a sound mind and this is what a sound mind does. It gives you solid wisdom to live and fight by.

Your life is worth living to the fullest. You were not created to be tormented by fear or any of fear's friends. You were created to enjoy the joy of the Lord, His power, His love, and a sound mind from God. You have these as gifts in you. Now receive and walk in them!

One of the marks of Satan's interference in your life is that your mind is darkened and unstable. When Jesus would cast demons out of people, those people would return to a sound mind or regain their right mind.

> *Luke 8:35 And [people] went out to see what had occurred, and they came to Jesus and found the man from whom the demons had gone out, sitting at the feet of Jesus, clothed and in his right (sound) mind.*

The Spirit of God gives you a sound mind when you believe God's provision of this for your own life.

Here is a summary of the triple threat you have in defeating the spirit of fear. The antidote to the spirit of fear is the Spirit of power, love and a sound mind. These three are administered to you by the Holy Spirit. The Holy Spirit is our Helper and our friend and we want to take advantage of His many benefits.

You are loved by God. Never, ever forget that truth!

Fearless Actions

1. What do you think of when you hear that you have the Spirit of power, love and a sound mind? Do you believe that it's true? _____

   _____

   _____

   _____

   _____

2. Why do you believe what you believe? _____

   _____

   _____

3. Are you ready to live a life forever free from the spirit of fear? _____

   _____

   _____

   _____

4. What bold steps are you ready to take today? What things are you ready to do now that you have not done because you were afraid? _____

_____

_____

_____

_____

Meditation

Meditating on these scriptures will help to secure your mind on the matter of the Spirit of power, love and a sound mind.

- Zechariah 4:6 Then he answered and spake unto me, saying, This is the word of the Lord unto Zerubbabel, saying, Not by might, nor by power, but by my spirit, saith the Lord of hosts.
- Romans 8:14 For as many as are led by the Spirit of God, they are the sons of God.
- Galatians 5:22 But the fruit of the Spirit is love, joy, peace, longsuffering, gentleness, goodness, faith.
- 1 Peter 1:22 Seeing ye have purified your souls in obeying the truth through the Spirit unto unfeigned love of the brethren, see that

ye love one another with a pure heart fervently.

- Isaiah 26:3 Thou wilt keep him in perfect peace, whose mind is stayed on thee: because he trusteth in thee.
- Matthew 22:37 Jesus said unto him, Thou shalt love the Lord thy God with all thy heart, and with all thy soul, and with all thy mind.
- Ephesians 4:23 And be constantly renewed in the spirit of your mind [having a fresh mental and spiritual attitude].

Chapter Ten

Highly Successful Habits of the Fearless

"You success hinges on your ability to receive and process the tools you've been given." - **Fiona Pyszka**

"I therefore, the prisoner for the Lord, appeal to and beg you to walk (lead a life) worthy of the [divine] calling to which you have been called [with behavior that is a credit to the summons to God's service" -
Ephesians 4:1

Anyone who is successful has a pattern that can be identified. Their life is a record of how they've behaved towards people and how they've accomplished their purpose in life.

There is no other life that shows a more fearless pattern than Jesus'. His life exuded the confidence of fearlessness that we can all strive to attain. Let's take a look at how He demonstrated His fearlessness towards Satan, men, and nature.

Face-to-Face Confrontation

Jesus had a face to face encounter with Satan in the wilderness.

Luke 4:3 And the devil said unto him, If thou be the Son of God, command this stone that it be made bread.

4 And Jesus answered him, saying, It is written, That man shall not live by bread alone, but by every word of God.

Jesus' response was the written word of God. His first response to Satan set the stage for His future encounters with Satan and demons.

Jesus did not spend time talking with Satan. He did not try to persuade him with multiple scriptures. Instead, Jesus spoke one scripture and ended the effect of Satan's temptation to Him.

When Satan presented another temptation, Jesus responded again with only one scripture from God's Word.

Jesus demonstrated to you that your answer to Satan and demons should not be conversations. Let your word be the last word of an exchange; don't leave the devil with vague answers. Be firm and quote the scriptures as they are written. Jesus overcame all three of Satan's temptations.

Your knowledge and expression of scriptures should grow in conversation with God. As you converse with God, speak His Word back to Him because He likes to hear that you know His Word. It shows that you are paying attention and building your relationship with Him. It is similar to a marriage relationship when you recall to your spouse a phrase or request that they have spoken. It makes them feel acknowledged.

God is interested in building a lasting relationship with you; therefore, use your knowledge of scripture as you talk with Him, or do His work. Stop having conversations with Satan or his ambassadors.

Habit One: Always speak directly to fear with the word of God and walk away.

Fear is a bully that always wants the last word. Don't let it trick you. Instead, speak directly to it and walk away.

Doing Good

Jesus did something else consistently. He always went about doing good. His goal whenever He traveled to different places was to make it better for the people after He left. We see this time and again in the New Testament stories of Jesus. The book of Acts says it best.

> *Acts 10:38 How God anointed Jesus of Nazareth with the Holy Ghost and with power: who went about doing good, and healing all that were oppressed of the devil; for God was with him.*

Jesus never feared when He went to different towns and encountered demons. This is because He was confident in the power of the Holy Spirit that worked in Him. He believed in God who anointed Him, and He understood the value of what He was doing for people. He realized that doing good was not just something that felt good to the doer, but it could be life or death for the receiver.

Habit Two: Be fearless enough to do good for people you encounter. Stop being afraid of people. Instead, offer your gifts and abilities to help them.

Jesus was very diligent about doing the word of His Father. The good that Jesus did for people was the result of the work of His Father. Jesus executed God's good works well. If you are a Christian then you have something good to offer the people you encounter, so release the good in you.

Provision

Feeding over 5,000 people was not a big problem for Jesus. He even used the occasion to test his disciples as part of their training with Him. Jesus demonstrated how His Father takes care of people who follow Him. We see in this passage how Jesus had been teaching a large crowd all day and in the evening He wanted them to be fed before leaving.

> *John 6:9 There is a lad here, which hath five barley loaves, and two small fishes: but what are they among so many?*
>
> *10 And Jesus said, Make the men sit down. Now there was much grass in the place. So the men sat down, in number about five thousand.*
>
> *11 And Jesus took the loaves; and when he had given thanks, he distributed to the disciples, and the disciples to them that were set down; and likewise of the fishes as much as they would.*
>
> *12 When they were filled, he said unto his disciples, Gather up the fragments that remain, that nothing be lost.*

Jesus was never accused by His disciples of being a bad planner and a terrible leader because of situations like this. Even though Jesus did not have a project management plan for feeding the thousands, He was always prepared for the needs of His ministry. He prepared by being in tune with His Father. Jesus would pull Himself aside and pray all night. This was His way of preparing for big exploits.

> *Luke 6:12 And it came to pass in those days, that he went out into a mountain to pray, and continued all night in prayer to God.*

Jesus never planned how to do something, yet He was always ready, in and out of season. He exemplified the fearlessness of overcoming obstacles and life's unexpected events.

Habit Three: Spend your time staying in tune with the Father so that you are ready to face any challenge life may present. Don't spend your time preparing for "what ifs." Live as if you have open access to the solution to any problem.

Jesus did not get caught up in figuring out what He was going to do because He sought first the Kingdom of God (Matthew 6:33).

The Ultimate Habit

The habit responsible for Jesus' greatest success against Satan was His obedience to the Father. He accomplished flawlessly what Adam and Eve failed to achieve. He fulfilled the ultimate plan that God has established for man: the plan for man to willfully obey His Word. Adam and Eve disobeyed God's Word and the spirit of fear showed up immediately.

> *Genesis 3:6-10 And when the woman saw that the tree was good for food, and that it was pleasant to the eyes, and a tree to be desired to make one wise, she took of the fruit thereof, and did eat, and gave also unto her husband with her; and he did eat.*
>
> *⁷ And the eyes of them both were opened, and they knew that they were naked; and they sewed fig leaves together, and made themselves aprons.*
>
> *⁸ And they heard the voice of the LORD God walking in the garden in the cool of the day: and Adam and his wife hid themselves from the*

presence of the LORD God amongst the trees of the garden.

⁹ And the LORD God called unto Adam, and said unto him, Where art thou?

¹⁰ And he said, I heard thy voice in the garden, and I was afraid, because I was naked; and I hid myself.

In verse 7 it says, "And the eyes of them both were opened, and they knew that they were naked." Their knowledge obtained through obedience to Satan did not bring joy, but shame. They were afraid of each other's nakedness, so they put a barrier between each other. Then they put a barrier between themselves and God. Verse 10 shows that their response to the presence of God was fear. The knowledge they acquired through following instructions from Satan was to hide from and be afraid of God. WOW! What a trap. This is still happening today. People are afraid and hiding from God. God created mankind, and yet Satan has convinced people that God is someone to hide and be protected from. Satan is the one that you should hide from and be protected from.

Jesus had a different response to Satan's attempt to give Him instructions. Luke tells us in his gospel that Jesus overcame Satan's instructions with God's Word (Luke 4). Jesus did not let Satan's intimidation trap Him into defending God's purpose for sending Him to earth. Jesus was not here to have conversations with or debate Satan and his cohorts. Jesus was here to be crucified on the cross and then be raised again for our new eternal life.

Jesus fulfilled all of His assignments from the Father, and met all of His Father's expectations. Jesus expressed that He fulfilled these purposes of God willfully.

> *John 10:17 For this [reason] the Father loves Me, because I lay down My [own] life—to take it back again.*
>
> *[18] No one takes it away from Me. On the contrary, I lay it down voluntarily. [I put it from Myself.] I am authorized and have power to lay it down (to resign it) and I am authorized and have power to take it back again. These are the instructions (orders) which I have received [as My charge] from My Father.*

Satan did not make Jesus die on the cross for our sins; Jesus did it willfully. Jesus did not allow Satan to dictate when He died. He chose the time and He chose how based on His obedience to the Father. We know this because there was another time when the people tried to kill Jesus.

> *Luke 4:29 And rising up, they pushed and drove Him out of the town, and [laying hold of Him] they led Him to the [projecting] upper part of the hill on which their town was built, that they might hurl Him headlong down [over the cliff].*
>
> *30 But passing through their midst, He went on His way.*

Jesus fearlessly protected His life so that He could finish what the Father started in Him.

Habit Four: Be obedient to God by fearlessly activating His power in you to protect yourself from Satan's plans to kill or stop you from fulfilling God's purposes in your life.

The Spirit of God

As we've established, fear is a spirit. Your natural man will never defeat the spirit of fear long term. You may overcome individual fears or phobias by lots of toil and intentional thinking; however, there is only one way that the spirit of fear can be neutralized from affecting any area of your life. How? You must have the same Spirit that Jesus had.

> *Isaiah 11:2 And the Spirit of the Lord shall rest upon Him—the Spirit of wisdom and understanding, the Spirit of counsel and might, the Spirit of knowledge and of the reverential and obedient fear of the Lord—*

The Spirit of the Lord was the key to Jesus' overcoming power. He had God's power to empower Him as He operated on this earth. The key to His operation in the power of God was to know whose instructions to obey and whose instructions to reject.

> *John 5:19 So Jesus answered them by saying, I assure you, most solemnly I tell you, the Son is able to do nothing of Himself (of His own accord); but He is able to do only what He sees the Father doing, for whatever the Father does is what the Son does in the same way [in His turn].*

Jesus made it clear that there was only one Spirit that He would mirror, and that was the Spirit of God,

His Father. Jesus was not interested in following any other spirit, including His own feelings.

> *Luke 22:42 Saying, Father, if You are willing, remove this cup from Me; yet not My will, but [always] Yours be done.*

Jesus surrendered to the leading of the Spirit through immediate obedience. He did not wait around until His flesh could decide whether or not He felt like doing what God wanted today Him to do. Everything that Jesus did had impeccable timing in accomplishing God's ultimate plan for mankind. Jesus would not even change God's schedule to accommodate His friends.

> *John 11:5 Now Jesus loved Martha, and her sister, and Lazarus.*
>
> *⁶ When he had heard therefore that he was sick, he abode two days still in the same place where he was.*

These were Jesus' friends who sent for Him to come and pray for their dying brother, Lazarus. Jesus did not quickly leave where He was to run in panic to heal Lazarus quickly so he wouldn't die. Instead, Jesus finished what He was doing because that was the assignment the Father wanted Him to do and finish. Then He went to Lazarus. Jesus was not afraid of death, but He confronted death as He raised Lazarus from the dead. He knew He had the victory over death.

Jesus conquered death in others by bringing them back to life because of the power of the Holy Spirit. The same Spirit that He knew would later raise Him from the dead also.

Habit Five: Be led by the Holy Spirit in your everyday life. Don't let fear move you to action; let the Holy Spirit's leading move you.

Being led by the Holy Spirit identifies us as children of God.

> *Romans 8:14 For as many as are led by the Spirit of God, they are the sons of God.*
>
> *15 For ye have not received the spirit of bondage again to fear; but ye have received the Spirit of adoption, whereby we cry, Abba, Father.*
>
> *16 The Spirit itself beareth witness with our spirit, that we are the children of God:*

The spirit of fear represents bondage. Jesus walked free from every kind of bondage, from every evil spirit, and from Satan. The spirit of fear is from Satan, never forget that! Jesus rejected Satan's seeds from being planted in Him. He did this by always obeying the Spirit of God.

In Conclusion

The agenda of the spirit of fear is to stop you from fulfilling your divine purpose on earth. Its goal is to paralyze you in key areas of your life that are required for you to move in so that your purpose for God can be accomplished. The spirit of fear will try to kill, steal from, and destroy you. Just having one of those destructive forces operating in your life is enough to delay the plan God has for you.

The spirit of fear operates by opportunity. When you give opportunity for it to have access to your mind, body, and spirit, it will take root and have residence as a chief advisor. As an advisor, it will decide whether you are capable, experienced enough, able, or wise enough to do something that God has asked you to do. It will become your résumé reader to your mind. It alerts you to all of your defects and past sins and warns you of the response people will have if you were to dare attempt an instruction from God.

The spirit of fear can cause you to see people as "objects" to be afraid of instead of people you can help or learn from. It is said that people are more afraid to speak in public than to die. How sad! People would rather die than stand in front of a group and share with them their knowledge and expertise that God has freely blessed them with. The spirit of fear is the leader of this type of behavior.

Praise God, there is an antidote for this thief of dreams, this robber of purpose, this destroyer of lives. The antidote is the Spirit that comes from God. You can be led by God's Spirit, walk in His ways, and be empowered for greatness.

It is my desire that this book has opened your eyes to the possibilities of being fearless. I pray that you will be able to accomplish with excitement and authority all that God has sent you here to do.

Now identify your progress in this mission of fearlessness. Record what you've accomplished and rejoice that you've won victory over the spirit of fear. Do it now!

Fearless Actions

1. I am now fearless in these areas of my life:

    _____

    _____

    _____

    _____

    _____

    _____

2. I will never let fear intimidate me again in these areas: _____

    _____

    _____

    _____

    _____

    _____

    _____

    _____

3. This is my strategy for always denying the spirit of fear access to my life: _____

    _____

    _____

    _____

Meditation

- Psalm 27:3 Though an host should encamp against me, my heart shall not fear: though war should rise against me, in this will I be confident.
- Psalm 46:2 Therefore will not we fear, though the earth be removed, and though the mountains be carried into the midst of the sea.
- Psalm 56:4 In God I will praise his word, in God I have put my trust; I will not fear what flesh can do unto me.
- Psalm 118:6 The Lord is on my side; I will not fear: what can man do unto me?
- Proverbs 19:23 The fear of the Lord tendeth to life: and he that hath it shall abide satisfied; he shall not be visited with evil.
- Isaiah 35:4 Say to them that are of a fearful heart, Be strong, fear not: behold, your God will come with vengeance, even God with a recompense; He will come and save you.
- Isaiah 41:10 Fear thou not; for I am with thee: be not dismayed; for I am thy God: I will strengthen thee; yea, I will help thee; yea, I will

uphold thee with the right hand of my righteousness.

- Lamentations 3:57 Thou drewest near in the day that I called upon thee: thou saidst, Fear not.
- Joel 2:21 Fear not, O land; be glad and rejoice: for the Lord will do great things.
- Matthew 10:26 Fear them not therefore: for there is nothing covered, that shall not be revealed; and hid, that shall not be known.
- Luke 12:7 But even the very hairs of your head are all numbered. Fear not therefore: ye are of more value than many sparrows.
- Luke 12:32 Fear not, little flock; for it is your Father's good pleasure to give you the kingdom.
- Hebrews 13:6 So that we may boldly say, The Lord is my helper, and I will not fear what man shall do unto me.
- 1 John 4:18 There is no fear in love; but perfect love casteth out fear: because fear hath torment. He that feareth is not made perfect in love.

Prayers for You

Prayer of Salvation

You can change your life by following Jesus, making Him your Lord and Savior. Man is born into sin and needs a Savior to redeem him back to God. Jesus came to take your sins and connect you back to your Father, God. He became your Savior. If you have never made Jesus the Lord of your life or accepted Him as your Savior, then this is your moment. Say this prayer with me:

Heavenly Father, in the name of Jesus, I present myself to You. I pray and ask Jesus to be Lord over my life. I confess that I am a sinner, and I need salvation. I receive Jesus as my salvation. I believe it in my heart, so I say it with my mouth: From this moment on I make Jesus the Lord over my life. Jesus, come into my heart. I believe right now that I am saved, I say it now: I am reborn. I am a Christian. I am a child of Almighty God. Amen.

Scriptures

John 3:16 For God so greatly loved *and* dearly prized the world that He [even] gave up His only begotten (unique) Son, so that whoever believes in (trusts in, clings to, relies on) Him shall not perish (come to destruction, be lost) but have eternal (everlasting) life.

Prayer for Release from the Spirit of Fear

I have prayed this over my own son, Gabriel, who was gripped by the spirit of fear. He has been set free and is now bolder than I've ever seen him. Praise God! You can be free too. So let's pray together.

In the name of Jesus and with the blood of Jesus, I command the spirit of fear to take its tentacles off of me right now. I give the spirit of fear no access to my mind, my body, or my spirit. I commit and put myself under the leading and guidance of the Holy Spirit. I speak that the blood of Jesus covers and protects me right now. My heart is in tuned with the frequency of God's Words and another voice I will not follow. I send far away from me the spirit of fear and I put my spirit on high alert to always listen to and follow the instructions of God Almighty. In Jesus' Name I pray, Amen!

Praise God! Now rejoice that you are free from the grip of the spirit of fear over you and in your life. You rejoice now by thanking God for His freedom.

From this day on you must change habits that have been in your life to accommodate fear. For my son, this was a critical step in keeping fear away. If fear tries to come back on you, you must resist immediately! Do not entertain any ideas that you were not set free. This is critical! You must resist immediately so that you keep yourself free from any return of this form of intimidation in your life.

Don't forget to change any habit that you may have developed to accommodate fear. Some examples might be staying away from crowds, keeping a problem hidden from others, not wanting to meet new people, the list goes on. Break the cycle today! **You are FEARLESS!**

Contact us:

If you received Jesus as your Savior, we want to hear about it. Contact us at:

fionap@fionainc.com

717-917-8101

For more information about Fiona Inc, visit us at our website, www.fionainc.com. While there, check out our free resources available to you. You may also purchase teachings and other valuable information.

Fiona also meets one-on-one with clients to help them further develop and pursue their purpose. If you would like to setup your own personalized session, email us for details.

If the information in this book has changed your life, we want to hear about it. So contact us today!

Visit us on Facebook to share your experience:

http://www.facebook.com/discoverfionainc Don't forget to hit the LIKE button.